Habitat
and
Technology

HABITAT
AND
TECHNOLOGY

The Evolution of Hunting

Wendell H. Oswalt
University of California, Los Angeles

HOLT, RINEHART AND WINSTON, INC.
New York   Chicago   San Francisco   Atlanta
Dallas   Montreal   Toronto   London   Sydney

To the maker of man—
THE STICK

Preface

Surprising, startling, perplexing, annoying, aggravating, virtually incom-prehensible. These are the words which first come to mind when I think about the ways in which anthropologists traditionally have approached the broad-scale study of material culture. The lifeways of all peoples quite literally are based on their manufactures, and yet there are no integrated, comprehensive studies of these productions in cross-cultural terms. How can it be that museums are filled with marvelous collections of material culture which gather dust, as do their curators who write about minutiae but never venture to compare their holdings for one people with those of another as integrated wholes? How can it be that paleoethnographers (commonly known as archaeologists) never systematically study information about material culture collected by ethnographers? Instead they draw disjointed analogies between their finds and certain data in ethnographic reports. Why is it that thousands of volumes have been published as a vast archive of in-formation about the manufactures of aboriginal peoples, and yet they seldom are consulted except to locate an exotic example to make a particular point? Ethnologists and paleoethnographers have written many studies about the development of particular artifact types, but these works—in terms of any broad conceptual context—are largely eclectic or else badly dated and eclectic. In order to verify the forcefulness of these statements one need only consult any comprehensive textbook in the field of cultural anthropology which has appeared within the last twenty years.

Anthropologists agree about comparatively little, but none would con-test that humanness developed in a large measure because of man's ability to make things which we have come to call artifacts. Neither would it be denied that technological knowledge has progressed from simple to com-plex as production skills and human understanding about the nature of materials has accreted. In a word, artifact forms have evolved through time. Yet as amazing as it may seem, the only systematic evolutionary analysis of diverse artifacts by an anthropologist was advanced in 1858 by Lane Fox Pitt Rivers. Somewhat later, in 1877, Lewis H. Morgan relied heavily on material culture in his development of ideas about cultural evolution, but his approach was neither thorough nor systematic. During the present century no anthropologist has ventured to attack the problem of technologi-cal evolution in an integrated manner. I find this to be a dereliction of scholarly duty. Why? Because of all the evidence about man's past, it is artifacts alone which provide the greatest insight into the development of humanness. Anthropologists and others interested in the changes in human thinking during the past three million years would do well to think about the evolution of social organization, political life, or religion *after* they begin to comprehend the nature of progressive changes in artifact forms.

The first problem encountered in embarking on this venture centered on the nature of classifications, because the material culture taxonomies established by ethnologists are wholly inadequate for approaching the questions which I had in mind. It was obvious too that a number of precise steps had to precede assessing the manufactures of different peoples in comparative terms, and dealing with evolution in technology. First, it was necessary to isolate the universe for study and then to ask certain fundamental questions about it. Next, the forms had to be classified in the most effective manner possible, given the universe and the questions. It was at this point that the ramifications of the questions emerged with clarity. Technology emerged as the universe to be considered in its cross-cultural complexity and evolution. My first task was to devise a framework (a classification) to accommodate material culture. I sought to devise a taxonomy which would permit me to compare diverse forms of artifacts made by different peoples around the world and to arrange the artifact data in a manner which would offer improved understanding about the development of forms. Taxonomy-building sometimes is judged as a sterile enterprise and is taken seriously by only a few persons. Yet we know too that a taxonomy may in itself be the first step toward refreshing approaches to subjects. The natural classification of Carl Linnaeus is the most notable case in point. One of my major goals has been to group items of material culture more comprehensively than has been achieved in the past.

Thus, this book has been conceived and written because of my lingering discontent with the manner in which ethnologists have considered and compared the manufactures of peoples in small-scale societies. I further deplore the barrenness of the conclusions which they have drawn. No means has been developed to compare the artifacts produced by different peoples in terms that are very insightful. What, for example, are the similarities and differences between the weapons made by the Arunta of central Australia, the Yahgan of Tierra del Fuego, and the Caribou Eskimos in the Barren Grounds of Canada? The more knowing ethnologists could offer many smooth generalizations about specifics based on an understanding of the artifacts involved, but their judgments would be at a very low level of abstraction. Furthermore, two different observers would never express the same interpretation. My aim is to replace qualitative evaluations in the comparison of manufactures with quantitative measurements of the comparative complexity of productions.

No people in the world are more enmeshed in the technological labyrinth than ourselves, and ethnographers in the United States have assembled a staggering amount of information about the manufactures of aboriginal peoples. It is ironic that in spite of these materially oriented interests no one has sought seriously to compare the technologies of hunters, fishermen, and collectors in an orderly manner. My goals are to offer statements about the comparative complexity of subsistence-oriented manufactures produced in small-scale societies, and at the same time to examine the evolution of technology from its beginnings.

W. H. O.

Appreciations

Without the prior existence of the culture core concept conceived by JULIAN H. STEWARD and the systematic approach to the comparison of technological forms derived by PHILIP L. WAGNER, this study could not have been attempted. Furthermore, without the trial applications of the taxonomy by VERA LUSTIG-ARECCO, refinement of the concepts developed in this work would have been long delayed and less exact. I also have profited greatly from the critical reviews of drafts of this manuscript by CARLETON S. COON, CLEMENT W. MEIGHAN, JAMES R. SACKETT, and GEORGE D. SPINDLER. Once again, and as usual, I deeply appreciate the positive value of the ideas and editorial assistance of HELEN TAYLOR OSWALT.

Contents

Habitat
and
Technology

Introduction

Within the broad and ever-expanding scope of anthropology, few topics are shunned. Book-length studies range in subject matter from fish hooks to sex or from myths to the plants used by man. At the present time, however, we find that thorough and systematic studies of material culture are confined almost entirely to the specialized analysis of excavated artifacts. Currently ethnologists, and to a lesser degree ethnographers, tend to avoid systematic studies of material culture. There was a time, especially between 1850 and 1920, when a great deal of expense and energy was expended to collect and analyze the manufactures produced by small-scale aboriginal societies. Innumerable publications appeared which not only described the forms themselves but offered comparisons on either a limited or a grand scale, but then interest in material culture faded rather abruptly. Most anthropologists, with the exception of paleoethnographers (archaeologists), have moved in directions which have excluded any serious attention being given to the manufactures of peoples. When artifacts are discussed, the stress usually has been in terms of the diffusion or independent invention of forms, the limitations posed on their production in various physical environments, the manufacturing methods, the physical isolation of peoples, or limitations imposed by psychological considerations. Although efforts along these lines at times have been revealing, a major drawback is that only isolated traits, complexes, or manufacturing processes are compared, resulting in fractured and fragmented studies. They do not permit technological wholes or integrated blocks of productions by particular peoples to be considered as comparative units.

My initial purpose is to isolate the most vital cluster of productions, the techno-economic forms which contribute most directly to day-to-day

1

survival among all men. The stress is on objects employed in order to procure food because this is a universal and a very basic need among men. These techno-economic productions are classified on the basis of the specific and general purposes which they served as well as in terms of the number of constituent components for each object. In this manner it becomes possible to compare the prime subsistence-oriented forms among diverse peoples.

A reconstruction of how and why this particular classification was formulated may serve as a means of indicating its limitations and potentialities. As an undergraduate at the University of Alaska, I was trained by anthropologists who were concerned mainly with arctic peoples. Their interest in ethnographic data centered largely on subsistence activities as integrated systems. When comparisons were made between cultures, the presentation was largely in terms of trait distributions in the manner of Kaj Birket-Smith (1929: pt. 2). My undergraduate reading included an article by C. van Riet Lowe (1945) about the Levallois technique in South Africa, and I was impressed by his effort to reconstruct the steps in tool production. His approach seemed important because manufacturing processes obviously are central to technological achievements. He indicated that by isolating the specific steps in artifact productions, forms could be clustered on the basis of their technological similarities and differences. In 1954, soon after reading this article, I excavated a site along Kaflia Bay on the Alaska Peninsula. I was alone there for about eight weeks, and when I became bored with digging, I attempted to manufacture stone tools like those I recovered. These efforts gave me a far greater appreciation of the steps required to produce particular forms. When preparing the Kaflia site report, I organized the descriptive material in hierarchical units based on the steps required in manufacturing artifacts from various materials (Oswalt 1955). To my knowledge the site report did not make a positive impression on anyone; in fact, the only response which I recall was extremely negative.

For a number of years I set aside the problem of how to order excavated recoveries in a more fruitful manner. As I began to teach ethnography courses, I found that my approach was the same as that of my instructors. The stress was on subsistence patterns of particular peoples, and comparisons were largely in terms of trait complexes whose similarities and differences around the world were explained, rather vaguely, in terms of diffusion and independent invention. I then read an article by Ruth Bunzel (1938) in which she discussed the qualities of natural materials in terms of solids, flexibles, and liquids. This division struck a responsive chord in terms of my Kaflia report. In 1963 James VanStone and I dug a historic Eskimo site in western Alaska, and in our report we were faced with the task of presenting excavated recoveries and ethnographic descriptions in an integrated manner (Oswalt and VanStone 1967). The effort was an inelegant failure. Yet it did begin to focus my attention on developing a descriptive framework which would accommodate ethnographic data systematically and at the same time have pertinence in the interpretation of excavated finds. In writing a book about Alaskan Eskimos, I organized the information about manufactures in terms of the qualities of raw materials in a rather mechanical but not entirely dissatisfying manner (Oswalt 1967:146–157). It was at this time that I began to classify all the artifacts produced by specific Eskimo groups in terms of the raw materials involved as well as the number of components or parts per artifact.

My efforts to derive a cross-cultural taxonomy for manufactures became more feasible after I considered Julian H. Steward's concept of cultural core (Steward 1955:37) and concentrated on techno-economic forms. A book by Philip L. Wagner (1960) was suggested to me by Daryl Maddox, and reading it was an important step forward. Wagner's classification of manufactures by functional form provided a highly useful means for separating various techno-economic artifacts into smaller units. My next step was to ask a research assistant, Vera Lustig-Arecco, to analyze the techno-economic forms, which I had come to call subsistants, for gatherers and incipient farmers around the world. The information was ordered within a modified form of the Wagner classification in terms of the number of components per form and the type of raw material involved —solid, liquid, or flexible. Before long it became apparent that stressing the qualities of the raw materials placed undue emphasis on the manufacturing processes which were no longer a central concern; therefore, the type of raw material was subordinated and utilized only in broad comparative summaries of taxonomic units. The next change was a decision to delete all peoples who were involved in farming so that the sample would be more homogeneous.

Retaining the number of components and the purpose of the artifact, I began anew. The manufactures of ten gathering peoples were analyzed in order to determine whether the revised classification was indeed operational, and I drafted a manuscript describing and exemplifying my analytical system. I then asked seminar students to apply the classification to diverse arctic peoples whom I had not considered previously. These students were confronted with problems that I had not encountered in my sample, and this required the revision of certain taxonomic units. Furthermore, they provided refreshing insight into ambiguities, and this led to other revisions. I also was fortunate enough to have Carleton S. Coon, James R. Sackett, and an anonymous reader study this manuscript draft.

The criticisms I received from Coon and Sackett were encouraging, while the anonymous reader made a blistering attack on the manuscript. In the face of this criticism I initially assumed the role of the hurt and misunderstood author, but the more I studied his comments, the more I realized that many of his barbs were well-aimed and valid. I came to the conclusions that superficial reasoning behind the formulation of the taxonomic units and a lingering confusion in the system had, at least in part, led to many of the anonymous reader's criticisms. The next step was to discard the original manuscript and write a fifty-page synopsis of the approach, taking into account the criticisms which I had received. This manuscript was read by Clement W. Meighan, and his favorable response encouraged me to write another book-length draft which in its essence is the text which follows.

In the two opening chapters I outline my purpose, my approach to technology, and introduce the taxonomic system. In the third through sixth chapters the subsistence-oriented forms used by diverse peoples are presented in terms of the classification, and limited generalizations as well as speculations are offered in the process. The purpose behind this organizational format is to lead the reader toward specific questions about the different categories of forms, questions which would have not presented themselves in so obvious a manner if the discussion had been in terms of inventories for only a few sample societies. It is incumbent on me to state why I have chosen particular peoples from which to draw illustrative examples. Initially it seemed quite clear that I should present the productions of societies which were "pure" and "untainted by exotic influence." To do this meant including only peoples who were well described early in their contacts with Europeans, Americans, or Euro-Americans. Thus, I sought aboriginal baseline ethnographic studies. An aboriginal baseline ethnography is made shortly following a people's first indirect, or direct, contact with complex, literate societies. Under ideal conditions an ethnographer would have been the individual to make the initial contacts, and he would have recorded faithfully all of the objects used by the people. A second, and less desirable, source of baseline data is an early observer's reconstruction of a group's life at the time of historic contact. In this instance the investigator conducts systematic interviews with knowledgeable persons about the manner in which they had been living and the objects which they had used during the aboriginal period. For my purposes, it would be best to have a complete inventory of techno-economic manufactures and details about the manner in which they were used, collected under the first condition mentioned, but this was rarely available.

The task of locating pertinent information was not as simple as had been anticipated. I was interested only in nonliterate peoples whose economy was based exclusively on hunting, fishing, and collecting foods. Thus, all farmers, herders, mounted hunters, and peoples who lived mainly by fishing were outside my area of interest, as were hunters and gatherers who practiced any horticulture at all, no matter how insignificant its contribution to their economic welfare might have been. Likewise, for any people to be considered, they must have maintained economic and political autonomy.

With these prerequisites in mind all of the peoples who occupied islands in the Pacific Ocean, including the Philippine Island Negritos, were eliminated because they were at least part-time farmers. With respect to Africa, it was obvious that most of the peoples on that continent were farmers or herders. Only the Bushmen of arid southern Africa, the Kindiga and Dorobo of east Africa, and the Pygmies of the Congo basin seemed to be likely prospects. I did not feel that I could include the Pygmies because of their economic dependence and their political attachments to adjacent Negro farmers. Most east African hunting peoples either were in the process of becoming farmers when contacted or else were subservient to and dependent on adjacent farmers before they were studied. The only satisfactory people were the Naron Bushmen. The South American groups were even more frustrating than the African. The peoples who seemed to be at the hunting-gathering level often had been destroyed before they were described, adopted European ways soon after historic contact, possessed at least some farming, or were inadequately described in the ethnographic literature. When people with these disqualifications were ruled out, the only remaining peoples were the Ona and Yahgan of Tierra del Fuego; the Yahgan were included. Australia posed no great difficulties since all of these people were hunters and gatherers, and many continued to follow their aboriginal ways until quite recently. Furthermore, some tribes, although not very many, are well described in the literature. The three selected for inclusion are the Arunta of central Australia, the Ingura of Arnhem Land, and the Pitapita of Queensland. I also included the Tasmanians and considered them residents of the general Australian region. Of people on the Eurasian landmass, the only gatherers who seemed to meet my requirements were some Yukaghir bands of Siberia and the Chenchus of India, but both were finally excluded because of the nature of their trade relations with adjacent peoples. For southeast Asia the Andamanese of the Andaman Islands are fully acceptable, but the data about the Semang were discarded because comprehensive information could not be isolated for a single group.

The best data are for North American peoples because they first were contacted in comparatively recent times and good studies of their material cultures were made. For these reasons more North American peoples are included in the sample than those from any other continent. Their weighted inclusion is justified not only on the grounds of available information, but also because of the wide variety of ecological settings in which they lived. The sample ranges from the littoral arctic Eskimos to northern forest-dwelling Athapaskan Indians, Paiute of an inland basin, and the coastal-desert dwelling Seri.

In drawing these introductory remarks to a close it must be emphasized that I am aware of, and have an appreciation for, the contributions made by numerous contemporary commentators about the emergence of technology and the ways in which to order forms as well as their attributes. The names of Lewis R. Binford, Richard A. Gould, Phyllis Jay, and Sherwood L. Washburn come to mind in this regard. Without for a moment detracting from the nature of these and other contributions, I have not discussed their specific findings because I seek to establish a particular overview of technology, and I prefer to avoid either agreeing with or contesting the conclusions drawn by others.

Part
ONE
The Approach

ONE

Nature Plus Man

Among animals man alone is capable of reflecting about the past of his species, and one of the most engaging of all his intellectual adventures is to study aspects of human beginnings. We can hope to learn only a small fraction of what reality might have been during man's genesis and early emergence, but this fact serves to heighten the challenge and invests the subject with intrigue. Man as a product of nature is at the same time much more, for he alone has dramatically altered the course of the earth's history with the objects that he has fashioned. In a very literal sense, too, the things which men have learned to manufacture have contributed immeasurably to the furtherance of both their human and inhuman qualities. A fundamental purpose of this book, elaborated in the opening chapters, is to develop a set of concepts which will encompass elementary developments in technology everywhere. Since this necessitates a discussion of "origins" and "beginnings" for a time far removed from the present, the subject is cast partially within an evolutionary framework. The concepts which emerge become the basis for the systematic comparison of manufactures among select peoples around the world, and their productions are ranked in terms of comparative complexity. The final goal, pursued in the closing chapter, is to isolate the most significant changes in the evolution of technology among hunters (for example, foragers, gatherers, hunters, fishermen, and collectors) from its origins until the rise of farming and pastoral economies about 10,000 B.C.

In considering manlike forms at the threshold of humanness over two million years ago, we have much more data about their anatomical characteristics than about their behavior. In various museums around the world there probably are enough bones of incipient humans to fill about two bushel baskets. These bones belonged to hominids who were bipedal, ground-dwelling beings—smaller renditions of ourselves. Their limbs and bodies were similar to our own, but their heads appeared much more ape-like and their brains were comparatively small. It is thought that their hands were capable of performing most of the manipulations which we perform today. Bones reveal much about physical morphology and, to a lesser degree, facilitate interpretive statements about how the animals functioned. Forms such as plant pollens and bones of other animals, if they are found in the same geological contexts as hominids, also tell something about the setting at that time, but nothing directly suggests the technological developments to come. Because of the physical characteristics of these beings, however, we may postulate certain technological categories which are likely to develop. For example, it may reasonably be presumed that those extraneous forms first held and used by man would be extensions of his own physical being.

ANATOMICAL AIDS

Anthropologists agree that emerging man was most likely omnivorous. Although some presume that meat predominated in his diet, in terms of the technological developments to come, it is necessary only to recognize that he ate both plant and animal products. Manlike beings obtained food by means of their own anatomy long before they began to employ extrasomatic forms. In order to qualify as an "anatomical aid" in this respect a morphological configuration must serve a specific function in obtaining food and must be analogous to some technologically simple form of instrument, weapon, or facility used in food-getting efforts later in time. For example, the teeth of emerging man probably cut in the manner of a weapon point, his hands might dig in the fashion of a stick, and fists could serve the battering function later achieved with a club. When an individual collected the leaves or berries from plants, his hands served as containers. Legs, teeth, arms, and fists in coordinated combination possibly were a deadly anatomical weaponry complex, comparable in certain respects to the hand-hurled spear to come. None of these retrodictions seems overextended; in a sense, anatomical aids were the "archetypes" of certain technological developments and may have led directly to the use of forms which were more efficient than their anatomical patterns.

It seems probable that ape-men became truly familiar with natural forms during food-getting activities. It was edibles that they first came to observe and manipulate. In order to survive they acquired foods, not just casually and out of passing curiosity, but carefully and for many hours each day. Hair and skin were torn free from animals in order to obtain meat, leaves were picked individually or in bundles, and berries, fruits, or seeds possibly were gathered with care. In addition, it is likely that eggs were retrieved from nests, toadstools picked from the ground, caterpillars lifted from leaves, rodents seized, and so on. This conjectured diet, or any other which might have been followed, offered experience in handling things. Given the presumed intelligence and curiosity of these beings, they would note further that a bent leaf might slowly assume its original form, that a twig would snap when twisted or might spring back into shape, and that grass pressed into a bundle tended to retain its clustered configuration when the pressure was released. We may assume that in each instance a cause and effect relationship gradually emerged in the observer's thinking and was reinforced frequently through manipulative experience. In this manner ape-men became familiar with the qualities of those raw materials which one day would become components in technology. Without such an era of experimentation, primarily related to food-getting, it would have been impossible for incipient humans to learn how to use raw materials in an effective and purposeful manner.

RAW MATERIAL CLUSTERS

In the era before man had altered his surroundings, the geographical features on earth, the plants and animals and all else, formed a truly natural setting. It is engaging to try and conceptualize the world of nature as it existed just before man began to make his presence felt. At that point in time the landscape and the creatures on it were not extremely different from those found in some areas at the present time. True, the terrain was not yet scarred by the action of glaciers of a later era, and the water systems differed from those to develop with the passage of more time; yet the earth was not too unlike its present-day form. The plant and animal populations were similar to those we find represented today in some localities; admittedly, many species which existed then are now extinct, but related forms usually remain. For example, mammoths and mastodons are gone, but elephants live on. We may therefore visualize the general landscape as it might have been before man became a part of it. The natural materials present during comparatively recent geological times would furnish the raw materials from which men would make forms called artifacts, and this process would lead to the development of something called culture.

Until recently, all objects made by men have been fashioned from materials which occurred on or very near the earth's surface. By grouping these natural materials according to their gross properties we begin to appreciate the use potential of different forms. No effort is made to limit this discussion to the materials which occurred in that sector of the world where men presumably developed first. Instead, materials will be discussed on a worldwide basis since sooner or later men would be exposed to such a range. The proposed classification contains only four cells: flexibles, solids, liquids, and plastics. In light of the variations a fourfold division is gross, but it is satisfactory to stress the significant differences and to illustrate the most important breaks. In the discussion to follow the materials are considered as they exist in an unmodified form and within a normal range of temperatures.

Flexibles are distinctly supple, pliant, and elastic; they characteristically give and bend rather than crack and break. They may be divided most conveniently and purposefully into those forms derived from plants and those of animal origin. The most important botanical contributions are from trees and include stems, wood, branches, bark, leaves, and roots. Supplementing these are vines, creepers, grasses, reeds, bamboo, and various species of bushes. Some woods, such as mesquite and oak, are flexible only in comparatively thin sections, and certain forms of bamboo are hard, consolidated masses. It is important in this regard to note that a material may vary in terms of its flexibility, particularly with respect to the thickness of the mass considered. These facts are very important and will be considered in due course. From animals such flexibles as skins, sinew, hair, wool, and feathers may be obtained. The faunal offerings are less diverse than are those found in the plant kingdom. It is worth noting also that geological formations rarely contribute natural materials which are flexible.

Solids occur as firm, largely unbending masses which by their very nature are neither elastic nor pliable. Examples from the animal kingdom include bones, teeth, tusks, antlers, horns, hooves, beaks, toenails, and shells of tortoises, turtles, mollusks, and eggs. In addition to certain forms of wood and bark, among plants we find nut shells and thorns. Geological formations yield stone, which occurs in varying degrees of hardness, as well as free copper, masses of soil, and even sand, since each individual grain is solid. Water frozen into ice or snow that is firmly packed also has the quality of a solid. *Plastics*, which are completely pliable substances, are comparatively rare; the most important are resins from living plants, asphaltum, sap, wax, and mud or moist clay. *Liquids* are derived in their greatest variety from animals and include urine, milk, blood, saliva, mucus, and oil; there are also plant juices, water, and petroleum oils.

These raw material clusters, because of their characteristics, have special pertinence in the beginnings of technology, the limitations of early achievements, and the possibilities of accomplishment. When considering the points to follow, it is helpful to imagine oneself living some two million years ago in an area in which highly diverse ecological settings might be near at hand; presume further that one is naked, alone, and without artifacts. Then think in terms of forms to use in obtaining food as well as materials which might serve to make tools or weapons. Without presuming that ancient man thought exactly as we do or that it is really possible to project ourselves backward in such a manner, the exercise does encourage more flexible thoughts about what might have occurred.

It seems very important that among flexibles the parts of plants provide a greater variety of materials with more possible uses than animal products. The degree of flexibility inherent in vines and grasses or the branches, bark, and roots of various trees is great. The possibilities of utilizing hair or wool from animals are far more limited, but sinew and skins approach the use versatility of certain plant products. Flexibles often serve best to hold other forms together; they function more effectively as binders than as items to be used alone. The number of natural flexibles which might be employed as containers is limited to such forms as leaves or bamboo sections. Again, natural flexibles which have the potential for direct and unmodified use as weapons or instruments are few in number; a stout stick is an obvious example, for it could be employed for digging, dislodging, battering, or spearing.

Compared with natural flexibles, solids have a narrower range of potential use. Solids such as stones or the long bones from animals could have served as bashers and batterers or in some instances as missiles. Cutting functions could be performed with teeth from carnivores or rodents by using them either intact in a mandible or as free forms; the sharp edge of a bivalve shell might serve as a knife. Most solids, however, would be of comparatively limited utility without some purposeful modification of their mass prior to use. From these observations we come to realize that few natural objects are capable of cutting. At the same time, some stone has great potential for being made into cutting blades because of the sharp edges that fracturing could produce on it.

Given the viscosity of plastics and liquids, they seldom could have stood as finished products among the earliest of men. The most likely function of plastics was as binding substances. Liquids may have been used during the processing of forms, but they rarely stood alone as finished products. Flexibles and solids were the key clusters of materials for making things.

All human environments contain plants, animals, and geological formations, and within each a diversity of raw materials is to be found. No known habitable setting lacks a raw material cluster, and yet because no ecological setting includes a complete range of forms, environments inherently limit manipulative possibilities. Given the distinct characteristics of each raw material cluster, it was essential for protohumans to have had considerable experience handling different materials within each group before successful utilization could possibly have occurred.

NATUREFACTS

In order to survive all animals must possess anatomical characteristics which make it possible for them to obtain and consume food. The wolf is fleet of foot, and with sharp canine teeth it rips the flesh of another animal in order to reduce it to food. The prehensile qualities of its trunk make it possible for an elephant to tear plant foods free and to transfer them into his mouth. The hands of a gibbon and the bill of a hawk serve similar procurement and associated intake functions. The creatures involved in these examples, through the interplay of morphology, physiology, instinct, and learning, are unto themselves sufficient in their food-getting efforts. In each instance somatic configurations which are inherent in the animal's form are called into play. The parts of a worm which make possible the obtaining of food may be judged as elementary and those of a seal as complex, but irrespective of this distinction, each creature is self-contained and most often self-sufficient.

An elaboration on physical attributes is involved when a creature develops extrasomatic means to obtain food or otherwise further its survival. Objects extracted from their natural setting and subsequently used without modification will be termed *naturefacts*. To withdraw something from the environment and to employ it as an extension of oneself is an activity which we do not expect of most life forms. It has been done, however, by a few insects, birds, and mammals; in each instance something which occurs in the creature's environment is extracted from a natural context and put to use without physical modification. In all probability, naturefact usage is an instinctive response for some species, but more commonly it appears to have been learned.

Two different species of wasps (*Ammophila urnaria* and *A. Yarrowi*) in the midwestern United States have been recorded as users of tools. An adult will find a pebble, use its mandibles to hold the pebble, and with it pound dirt into a nest (Peckham and Peckham 1898:22–23; Williston 1892:85). A satin bower-bird (*Ptilonorhynchus violaceus*) of eastern Australia will hold charcoal, berry pulp, or another substance in its beak until it has mixed with saliva; the mixture then serves as a paint which is applied to the interior of a bower (Chisholm 1954:381; Marshall 1960:207). It is far more common, however, for the nonprimates to use

Figure 1–1. A solitary wasp using a pebble to pound down earth over its nest (from Peckham and Peckham 1898).

naturefacts in their food-getting activities. The Egyptian vultures (*Neophron percnopterus*) in Tanzania have been photographed during such a process. The vulture holds a small stone in its beak and stands next to an ostrich egg. He pelts the stone against the egg, and if the first stone does not succeed in breaking the shell, another may be found and used. The vulture may carry a stone as far as fifty yards in order to strike at an egg, even though this method of obtaining food is successful only about half the time (Goodall 1968:630–641). In widely separated areas of Australia the black-breasted buzzard (*Hamirostra melanosterna*) has been reported to drive an emu from its nest, pick up a stone or hard lump of earth in its claws, fly over the nest, and drop the missile to break the eggs so that it can consume their contents (Chisholm 1954:382–383). The southern sea otter (*Enhydra lutris nereis*) has a more complex pattern of tool use. This aquatic mammal, found along the Pacific coast of North America, may carry a large abalone, or a mussel, and a stone from the ocean floor to the surface. The otter rolls over on its back at the water surface, rests the stone on its chest, holds the shell in both paws, and pounds it against the stone anvil. In this manner the shell is broken and the meat retrieved. The same stone may be used to open more than one shell; possibly the sea otter holds the stone in an armpit during dives (Fisher 1939:28; Hall and Schaller 1964:287–298). The use of naturefacts among the wasps appears to be instinctive, but there is a suggestion that the stone usage is taught to young sea otters. The manner in which the birds acquired their use of naturefacts is not known.

Although captive apes and monkeys learn to use tools with little apparent effort, tool use among wild animals of these species is rare. In their natural habitat these animals handle objects during aggressive displays more often than for any other purpose. When threatened by men red spider monkeys (*Ateles geoffroyi*) may break off living or dead tree branches which weigh up to ten pounds and let them fall toward the in-

Figure 1–2. A chimpanzee stripped the leaves from a stick and inserted it into a termite nest (Courtesy of Baron Hugo van Lawick © National Geographic Society).

truder (Carpenter 1935:173–174). Reportedly too, howler monkeys (*Alouatta palliata*) snap off dead branches and drop them in the direction of an aggressor (Carpenter 1934:27). Gorillas (*Pan gorilla*) sometimes use branches in much the same manner, although they appear not to aim them (Schaller 1963:224–225), and orangutans (*Pongo pygmaeus*) may throw branches to the ground if they are being followed by a man (Schaller 1961:81). In all of these authenticated observations, the naturefacts were used in aggressive reactions (Hall 1968:134–138).

Among free-living primates apart from men, only chimpanzees (*Pan satyrus*) are known to employ naturefacts for obtaining food, and even among them such implement use is uncommon. Chimpanzees in Liberia have been reported to break palm nuts by placing a nut on one rock and hammering it with a second rock (Beatty 1951:118), whereas elsewhere in west Africa they have been known to poke a twig into a nest of bees to retrieve the honey which adheres to the stick (Merfield and Miller 1956: 45). Chimpanzees in Tanzania have been observed poking sticks into termite and ant nests. Numerous insects bite and hold onto the stick, which is then withdrawn and the harvest eaten. In preparation for this activity, chimpanzees have been observed selecting a stalk of grass, a section of vine, or a twig which they may break to about a foot in length. Furthermore, they may remove the leaves from such a twig or vine with their lips or fingers (Goodall 1965:440–443). To purposefully break a stick to a desired length or to strip away the leaves from a twig illustrates the process of artifact manufacture. These chimpanzees also collect leaves which they wad and chew to form a moist ball. The ball is stuck into a tree bole to soak up otherwise inaccessible water. After it becomes saturated, the sponge is removed from the hole, and the water is sucked from the leaves (Lancaster 1968:58–59). The modified probing sticks and wadded-leaf sponges made by chimpanzees are the only recorded examples of artifacts manufactured by nonhuman primates living under natural conditions.

As interesting as the naturefact usage among wasps and vultures, or the even more fascinating sea otter behavior, may be, it suggests little about artifact production as it developed among men. The nonhuman usages and productions are minimal and rare, and they appear to be uncorrelated with the intelligence of the species involved (Hall 1968: 132–134). As stressed by Phyllis C. Jay (1968:495) the latter observation should give pause to persons who attempt to correlate implement use and the brain size of the creatures involved. The artifacts produced by chimpanzees are somewhat more valuable as examples, for they are more clearly manufactured and offer at least a hint of what may be achieved by curious primates who are not very far removed from the human line.

Naturefacts probably were used by aborigines far more frequently than the ethnographic reports suggest. In all likelihood most observers did not participate fully enough in the day-to-day lives of the peoples whom they described to notice naturefacts in use; even if such forms were observed, their significance was easy to overlook. The Pitjantjatjara ethnography by Richard A. Gould (1969:82–83) is a notable exception since the author details naturefacts used by these aboriginal Australians in the western deserts. Gould termed naturefacts "instant tools" and wrote:

> the tool needed for a particular task was obtained from some natural object or material immediately at hand and after being used was discarded. It had no value except as a means of solving an immediate practical problem. In most cases there was no attempt to modify the natural material by trimming or shaping, although some of the hand-held stone scrapers acquired a distinctively concave edge through wear. Just by looking at most of the stones afterward it would be hard to tell that they had once been tools.

ARTIFACTS

Naturefacts must be considered separate and distinct from those objects which are manufactured; *artifacts* are forms created by withdrawing materials from their natural setting and modifying them in trifling or in remarkable ways. To break a branch from a tree and strip away the twigs for a particular purpose is to make an artifact. To strike one stone against another and derive a sharp-edged implement is a similar process, as is the plaiting of grasses to form a basket. In each of these examples learned skills are applied in order to produce the artifact.

No single artifact type is made by all peoples throughout the world. If one were, we would suspect that its manufacture was an instinctive response in man. It might be supposed that particular objects linked to such human physiological processes as eating, excreting, or menstruating occur everywhere, but this is not the case. All peoples do not eat with spoons, and the use of toilet paper, or even a reasonable substitute, is lacking in many societies. Furthermore, although most women around the world wear menstrual pads, even this form is not universal in distribution. In these terms no form of artifact made by humans is comparable to a bird's nest, a prairie dog's burrow, or a beaver's lodge, each of which is made by the members of species with instinct as the primary guide.

TECHNOLOGICAL DISCOVERIES

A discovery is the process of coming to realize the existence of something that previously was unrecognized. It may be very specific, such as finding a previously unknown planet in the heavens, or it may be a general concept, such as coming to understand the principle of gravitation. Before man could be launched on his many and diverse technological ventures, it first was necessary for him or his immediate precursors to have made many discoveries about the qualities of things in the natural world. These ideas need not have risen to a level of consciousness, however, and some unquestionably had begun unfolding long before the separation which would give rise to man. One was an implicit recognition of the *discreteness among forms*. This meant there was an awareness that a tree was a separate and isolatable entity which contrasted with a rock, an antelope, or another tree. Realization of this discreteness and of the differences among natural forms exists in many creatures other than primates. Along the same lines it was essential to discover the contrasting characteristics of natural substances as grouped in *raw material clusters*, which have previously been described. This was a giant step toward technological productiveness and came about as a result of food-handling among ape-men. Following this, another discovery completed the background for all future technological developments; it was the momentous step of removing a natural form from its setting for a planned purpose. *Use-removal* was a critical innovation because it gave rise to the employment of naturefacts and, through the handling of them, to a manipulative familiarity with materials.

The next step was a realization that naturefacts could be changed in form; this led to the development of the *reduction process*, the first method used to produce artifacts. This discovery was applied in changing a stick into a simple spear by making a sharp point at one end, flaking a stone to produce a knife, or converting a slab of bark into a container. Among the most basic artifacts were those comprised of a single component and formed simply by reducing the mass. Typical products of this development are the digging stick, simple shaft spear, or stone knife. The reduction process not only was critical in making one-component artifacts, but the same principle was involved in producing the components to be used in compound forms. In order to make a typical composite spear, a craftsman chipped a stone spearhead, cut and planed a shaft of wood, and reduced a piece of rawhide to strips for use as binding. Occasionally the reduction process was of a different nature, but was reduction nonetheless. For example, a handful of grass might be collected, which led to a reduction of the living mass of which it was a part; the wadded handful could be used to soak up honey from a bee's nest.

Once it was realized that natural forms could be removed and used for a purpose, the next step was to join more than one such object for greater effectiveness. Discovery of this, the *multiplication process*, had diverse ramifications. In essence it meant that components could be brought together as multiples in order to function more effectively than a single element or even in a manner which was impossible for a single-component form. For example, one stone could not be used to dam a stream, but an effective dam could be made by using multiple stones. In a similar manner many pieces of brush could be arranged into two converging lines to guide game toward concealed hunters. Another principle which is an aspect of multiplicity is termed the *duplication process*; this is a method of manufacturing replicas of a form component, such as making two similar points for attachment at the end of a weapon shaft. When duplicative parts function only as a unit and involve physical movement, as in a pair of scissors, the process is called *complementary necessity*. None of these methods of multiplication could exist, however, until the *conjunctive principle* had been discovered. This meant that two or more components could be joined physically with one another; this principle was applied in lashing a stone point to a spear shaft with a piece of rawhide.

These principles and processes became the enablers of technology. We then find that *amplifications of techniques* occurred in various media as craft skills were developed. Thus, woodworking technology was amplified as men learned to char, gouge, cut, scrape, bend, drill, and mortise wood, and the same was true of other raw materials, such as antler, bone, and stone. For example, two pieces of wood might be joined by overlapping and binding two components; alternatively, the joint might be scarfed or dovetailed. These techniques have developed as amplifications of woodworking methods. These differ from *design amplifications*, which are elaborations on a particular technological method. Design amplifications are seen in spearpoints of different appearance produced by a single set of techniques. For example, a spearpoint might simply be a long tapering point, might be barbed on one side, barbed on both sides, or have barbs supplemented with a separate point at the tip. *Quantum leaps* are distinct from technique and design amplifications because they are discoveries of major new technological ideas. The first manufacture of artifacts was a quantum leap, as was the first production of composite forms. Such momentous occasions rarely took place among hunters, but the resultant changes in material culture which did occasionally occur led to much more efficient use of human energy.

CULTURE

Certain phenomena found to occur among nonhuman species represent "infrahuman culture." The use-removal process was discovered by certain birds and by mammals such as the sea otter and chimpanzee. That some chimpanzees also discovered the principle of multiplicity is evidenced by their placing palm nuts between two stones in order to crack the nuts. Furthermore, certain groups of chimpanzees had learned to make two types of artifacts: the wadded grass, water-retrieving sponge and the stick modified to serve as a probe for termite and ant nests. The use of all of these forms probably was perpetuated through social learning rather than genetic transmission.

Anthropologists differ widely in their precise definitions of culture, but most would agree that the essence of the concept is found in the notion of learned behavior which is shared widely by the members of a society. John J. Honigmann (1959:11) lists activities, artifacts, and ideas as being the phenomena of which culture is comprised. Robert J. Braidwood (1963:38) states that culture "means the way the members of a group of people think and believe and live, the tools they make, and the way they do things." In any event, traditionally accepted as the earliest evidence of culture are manufactures, and the oldest known forms consistently have been made from stone. From all existing evidence we may presume that man was their maker, and thus we usually equate technology with man and with culture.

If in fact evidence for the production of technological forms is the only clear evidence for the beginnings of culture, then why is it that manufactures are largely ignored, or considered as secondary, in discussions about cultural differences among diverse aboriginal peoples at the time of historic contact? Admittedly some people have been judged as being in the Stone Age or an Age of Metals, but these and similar dividers are so gross that they are totally inadequate in most detailed studies. The major distinctions among peoples are normally based on contrasts in social or political institutions; yet these are as much as anything else reflections of a level of technology. My contention is that man is first and foremost a technological animal and that the major distinctions among lifeways should be made on the basis of manufactured forms. Thus, it basically is, and was, technoculture that made man what he is or is not. This is a critical point for understanding man in culture and will be elaborated at length in the closing chapter.

HUNTERS

Hunters are nonliterate peoples who were politically and economically independent when they were encountered first by Europeans, Chinese, and Euro-Americans, or by the members of other literate and complex societies. They subsisted by hunting, fishing, or collecting, and usually combined these subsistence activities. They may alternatively be called small-scale or tribal societies, gatherers, foragers, or primitive peoples. It is these societies that are considered in the presentation to follow. Information about the material culture of hunters will be utilized in two distinct ways. First, it will be used to draw analogies with possible early steps in the evolution of technology. Secondly, it makes possible an interpretation of the comparative complexity within material culture of different groups at an elementary economic level. In a presentation about the origins and early development of technology it may seem irrelevant to describe the ways of hunters as they were found at historic contact; I hope, however, to demonstrate that the opposite position is in fact more reasonable.

During the rise of anthropology the proposition that culture in general had evolved from simple to complex was accepted with conviction by such pioneers as Edward B. Tylor and Lewis H. Morgan. Their critics, however, soon demonstrated that an evolutionary taxonomy, such as that proposed by Morgan (1877), was based partially on unreliable ethnographic data and included inconsistent propositions; subsequently, evolutionary "schemes" fell into disrepute. Since World War II they have gained an ever-increasing acceptability as more intensive research has put them on a more firm empirical and conceptual base. It is not my purpose to detail either the pros and cons of such taxonomies in historical terms or the alternative frameworks for integrating sociocultural data. I have only a single point to make in this regard. Robert H. Lowie (1937:27), who was devoutly opposed to evolutionary classifications, nonetheless asserted, that "evolution is a positive fact in material culture." Thus, even a vigorous opponent of cultural evolution accepted the fact that the forms of artifacts changed through time from simple to complex.

We often have reports of aboriginal peoples making and using only artifacts of simple manufacture at the time of their first historic contact, but other peoples in different places were found to make complex forms. In technological terms, the simple forms of the one group would be judged as less evolved than those of the other. For example, aboriginal peoples on the island of Tasmania were described by explorers as making only two weapons, both of which were very simple in absolute as well as comparative terms. One, which served as a spear, was a long shaft of wood with a sharpened point, and the other was a short stick which was thrown at animals or used to club them. In another isolated area, the early historic Yahgan of Tierra del Fuego made spears tipped with stone points and harpoons with detachable, barbed heads. Clearly their weaponry was technologically more developed than that of the Tasmanians. Comparisons of this order make it possible to gain general insight into technological changes, but we cannot expect to achieve detailed precision without a more structured method of comparison. It is important, therefore, to set forth a taxonomy and apply it to an analysis of material culture. The comparisons developed in this text make it possible not only to identify the degree of relative complexity of any hunting group but also to draw analogies which clarify the steps in material culture evolution.

TWO

Taxonomy

No one has ever been bold enough to calculate the number of different artifact types which men have produced nor brazen enough to estimate the production totals. Rather clearly, however, it was only with the rise of cities about 5000 B.C. and again during the Industrial Revolution which began about A.D. 1760 that major surges occurred in the manufacture of different artifact types. In terms of all the different forms produced by present-day industrial nations, the production totals for hunters have been modest. Yet even when attention focuses on the evolution of manufactures among these peoples, the task of separating, sorting, and totaling is formidable. Given the difficulty of coping with this universe of forms in an effective manner, it seems the most reasonable approach would be to isolate that cluster of manufactures which encompasses the essence of all technological developments. The determination of this block of objects is not as difficult as it might first appear when two criteria are recognized as essential: the major categories must occur among all peoples and must be intimately linked with the most basic methods of survival.

In order to endure as a species it is essential for man to reproduce himself; this, the biological aspect of human continuity, is vital but is not a dimension of this study. Physical protection and the procurement of subsistence are the other essential aspects of human survival, and of these, procurement is the more fundamental. Men everywhere must obtain nourishment through food-getting activities, and since this requirement is fulfilled almost entirely through technological usages, the focal point of all subsequent discussions will be the food-getting technology.

THE PHYLUM SUBSISTANT

It is desirable, if not essential, to coin a word which will distinguish the objects used to obtain food from all other forms employed by man. The word proposed is *subsistant*, and it will mean any extrasomatic form which is used directly by man in his procurement of food. The term is derived from *subsist* meaning "to support with provisions," and the suffix *-ant*, meaning "the agent that performs a specific action or process." Ordinarily men are unable to survive for any reasonable length of time without bringing subsistants into play. Under normal circumstances subsistants were used by foragers nearly every day of their mature lives. Hunting spears, snares, honey-removing sticks, stones thrown at birds, clubs for braining seals, and fish nets all are subsistants. Excluded from consideration are housing, clothing, furniture, food processors, production tools, and so on. It is not for a moment suggested that only subsistant forms were important in furthering human survival in a very elementary manner. Certain other categories, such as production tools, also were critical, while in an environment such as the arctic, habitations and clothing were basic needs. Subsistants, however, were *universally essential* among people, irrespective of their geographical location or their relative level of development.

The concept of a "subsistant" as a vital category in a sense parallels the technological component of the cultural core concept advanced by Julian H. Steward (1955:89, 93). Both stress that certain blocks of materials are more important than others in culture and therefore in cross-cultural comparisons. A major obstacle in the systematic comparison of manufactures by different peoples has been the presumption that all artifacts should be considered as essentially equal in importance because each reflects cultural behavior. Paleoethnographers will make little headway in broad- or narrow-range comparisons without rejecting this approach, but to do so they must evaluate ethnographic collections carefully. Comparisons are bewildering when hairnets, diaper pads, houses, and spears are presented as being of much the same importance. It is little wonder that ethnologists have turned to tracing the distribution of particulars or to discussions about the evolution of limited complexes.

The subsistant category is designated as a phylum (Table 2–1) with representative types distinct from any other group of forms at the same taxonomic level. The subsistant phylum is the only one considered in this book, but other phyla could be isolated and categorized in a similar fashion. These might include military weaponry, structures, production tools, means for food processing, storage devices, bodily adjuncts, and so on. It is worthwhile to bear in mind that even though this discussion deals only with subsistants, the taxonomic approach to their presentation seems capable, through expansion, of accommodating the entire range of material culture.

SUBPHYLA

The subsistant phylum is divided into the subphyla of *naturefacts* and *artifacts*, based on distinctions which were discussed in the preceding chapter. Forms within the naturefact subphylum are technologically simpler than artifacts; as unmodified natural objects they are the most ele-

Table 2–1   Classification of the cultural phylum "Subsistant."

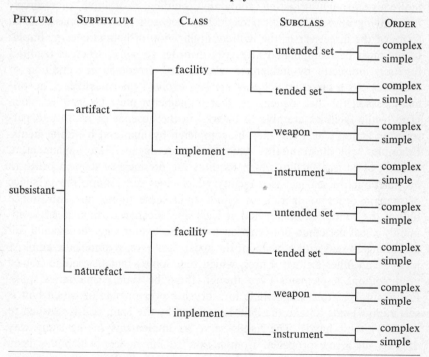

PHYLUM	SUBPHYLUM	CLASS	SUBCLASS	ORDER
subsistant	artifact	facility	untended set	complex / simple
			tended set	complex / simple
		implement	weapon	complex / simple
			instrument	complex / simple
	naturefact	facility	untended set	complex / simple
			tended set	complex / simple
		implement	weapon	complex / simple
			instrument	complex / simple

mentary extensions of anatomical aids. Types in the artifact subphylum are judged as having developed from archetypes among naturefacts. Above all else, this means that within any particular category of subsistant, the forms in the naturefact subphylum will be less developed technologically

than those of the artifact subphylum. Although artifacts evolved from
certain naturefacts, this does *not* imply that all naturefact usages have
comparable antiquity or that particular forms of naturefacts could not
have come into usage long after artifacts had developed in the same or
other orders. Instead, it is concluded that within the general evolution of
subsistants, naturefacts are technologically simpler than artifacts and that
in techno-developments they predate artifacts at any particular level.

CLASSES

Naturefacts and artifacts alike are subdivided into the classes of
implements and *facilities*. Implements are forms designed to apply human
energy directly in order to obtain sustenance; they impinge on and physically alter other masses. Facilities are designed to apply human energy
indirectly, through attracting, containing, holding, restraining, or redirecting a living mass. The critical distinction between these two classes is in
terms of the direct versus the indirect application of human energy. Implements must be manipulated manually in order to work, whereas facilities
function indirectly by influencing the nature, freedom, or condition of
creatures. As a class, implements are less evolved than facilities. The primary reason for this sequence is that implements must be handled when
used, while facilities are able to "work" in the absence of man or to perform an action which can then be completed by man and his implements.
Examples will illustrate this major point. A spear is an implement; a
hunting blind is a facility which requires the presence of man in order to
be functional; a seal net is a facility which does not require the presence
of man in order to operate. A blind could serve to provide subsistence
only if the concealed hunter had at least one effective weapon at his com-
mand; a seal net could not function unless the hunter who set it could kill
an entangled seal with a weapon; the spear, however, required the employment of no other artifact. Lures, which function as facilities, could not be
used without implements even though these be simply anatomical aids.
For example, a man might hide in a brush bower outside of which bait is
set; a crow lands to take the bait, is grabbed by the man, and is crushed to
death with his hands. The hands serve as implements in the same way
as does an arrow propelled from a bow to kill a deer which has been
lured. A pitfall is a facility which might not require the presence of man
in order to function, but a hunter may not be able to subdue the quarry
without implements. Spears arranged with their points upright in the bottom of a pitfall would be an even more developed use of implements and
facilities, because in this instance forms from two classes are combined in

their usage. Thus, it is reasoned that just as naturefacts as a class of forms are simpler than artifacts, implements as a class are less evolved, less complex conceptually, and were conceived earlier than facilities.

SUBCLASSES

Among implements, the subclasses of *instruments* and *weapons* are identified. Instruments are employed to perform tasks in which the living mass impinged on is incapable of significant motion. Although most often this means plant products or lower species of animals, in certain cases it applies to inert game animals. Edibles that do not move appreciably are procured most often with the aid of instruments; examples include the use of a stick in order to remove honey from a bee's nest, dig up mollusks, or remove roots from the ground. Weapons are designed to kill or seriously injure creatures which are capable of significant motion at the time the forms are brought into play. Weapons are employed against antelope, deer, kangaroos, rabbits, seals, and so on. It is reasoned that as a subclass instruments are simpler, older, and less developed than weapons because instruments are more elementary extensions of anatomical techniques.

Facilities are divided also into two subclasses, *tended* and *untended* *sets*. Tended sets are those which require the presence of one or more persons in order to function. For example, a hunting blind served the purpose for which it was designed only when a man was concealed in it. The same applied to the manipulation of a dip net at a fishing spot or the use of a lure when fishing. Untended sets by contrast did not require the action of a person in order to function; in theory, they "worked" constantly. A snare set for hares, a pitfall for taking caribou, or a fish weir and trap in combination did not require the man or men who made them to remain at the site in order to take fish or game. It is reasoned that as a subclass tended sets are conceptually simpler than those which are untended. A subsistant which functions in the absence of man is the most sophisticated of possible usages.

ORDERS

The next taxonomic unit is the order level. Within each subclass the orders identified are *simple* and *complex*. A simple form retains the same physical appearance before, during, and after it is brought into play. Often a simple form is composed of a single component or part. An example among instruments would be a digging stick with which to remove roots from the ground. A digging stick does not significantly change its form from the time it is made until it is discarded. A simple form of weapon would be a spear made from a shaft of wood pointed at one end. An example of a simple tended facility would be a blind made from brush to conceal a hunter; it would be stable in form throughout the period of use. A complex instrument, weapon, or facility always has more than one component, and its parts change in their physical relationship to one another during use. For example, two sticks tied together near one end might serve as tongs to be used by a person for removing mussels from their bed. The tongs have three components, the two sticks and the lashing material; the components change in their physical configuration with one another while being used. Since the shellfish are not capable of motion, the tongs used to obtain them qualify as an instrument, and because the components must change their relative positioning in order to function, the form is complex. A toggle-headed harpoon is an example of a complex weapon. The harpoon head detaches from the shaft when the weapon strikes an animal, thus changing the harpoon's physical form, and the animal taken is a moving creature. A combination of fish weir and trap is a simple untended facility because it is stable in form as it guides fish. A spring-pole snare is an example of a complex untended facility. When the trigger is released by an animal, a noose tightens about it because of the action of the spring pole. Breakage, repairs, and wear patterns do not qualify as significant changes during operation; all three are secondary results of use. It is reasoned that simple forms arose before the complex ones because they are more elementary extensions of anatomical usage, have fewer components, and do not require the knowledge of any "mechanical" principle for their effective employment.

The orders "simple" and "complex" are of a different quality than the other taxonomic units which have been defined because they are used in an identical manner throughout the classification at the order level. It should be noted that a classification of material culture need not precisely parallel the binomial patterning found in taxonomies of natural species. In fact, there is one exceedingly good reason why an identical type of arrangement cannot be employed: material culture is not a "natural" system but one made by man and therefore requires an ordering of a different nature.

AIDS

Given the restrictive definition of subsistants as extrasomatic forms used *directly* to obtain food, it is quite clear that other forms might complement and supplement their usages. When considering the activities of hunters, it is necessary to distinguish three clusters of aids which are labeled as *natural, anatomical,* and *artifactual.*

Natural aids exist independent of man and were employed by him without any change in their innate characteristics. Natural aids differ from naturefacts because of their "living" quality. The most obvious example, and one of the most widespread food-getting aids, was fire. Brushland, grasslands, and forests were set on fire in order to suffocate animals or to drive them from concealment so that they might be killed with weapons. Vegetation also might be burned over in order to attract game to the tender plants that would appear during the next growing season or to harvest the new plants themselves. Animals often were asphyxiated by the smoke from fires built at the entrances of their burrows, while the nests of rats or birds might be burned and the bodies picked up afterwards. Water might on occasion serve as an aid; for example, it sometimes was poured down burrows to drown any animals trapped in them. In a sense geographical formations also served as aids; game could be driven over cliffs or into bogs. Dogs functioned as aids in many different contexts. They might be trained to kill large and small game or taught to track and corner animals so that they could be killed by a hunter. Some Eskimos used dogs to sniff out the breathing holes of seals on ice fields.

Anatomical aids are human physiological components employed in the procurement of food products in a direct or indirect manner. Direct anatomical aids include human hands or feet used in order to obtain food without the assistance of any extrasomatic forms. Collecting mushrooms or eggs, stripping grass seeds from stalks, picking berries or fruit are examples of hand retrieval. Shellfish might be felt with one's toes and picked up with them. Possibly the most important indirect anatomical aid was the use of the voice to imitate animal sounds. This might be done in order to lure species near enough to be killed with weapons or to lull them into a false sense of security as the hunter approached.

Artifactual aids are man-made objects employed to supplement subsistants in food-getting activities; they enable a forager to be more effective with his implements or facilities. The number of forms used in this manner is great, but a few examples will serve to illustrate their nature. A boat aided in the hunting of sea mammals or in the setting and tending of a fish net; snowshoes were worn when tracking moose in winter; riding a sled pulled by a dog team made it possible to reach distant hunting grounds; or a length of grass might be looped around both a tree and a man's body and tied, thereby enabling the man to climb a tree and reach game.

In assessing the complexity of subsistence activities, a knowledge of the range of aids employed by a people is extremely important. Among those with the most developed food-getting efforts, diverse aids were brought into play. When aids in any form are employed with subsistants directly in food getting, the usage is considered an *association*.

MEASUREMENT OF SUBSISTANT COMPLEXITY

It commonly is accepted, for rather good reasons, that the ape-like creatures whose descendants soon were to become men had forsaken tree dwelling in favor of ground living. In terms of present-day nonhumans they possibly were rather like baboons socially, but they more nearly approached some ancestral form of chimpanzee physically. Their maturation probably was prolonged, their capacity for play was great, and their degree of curiosity and intelligence was unprecedented. Small groups of these ape-men foraged food, used naturefacts, and then began to modify materials in the creation of artifacts. A critical stage was reached when a variety of forms were made and used habitually. As this process became elaborated, the ape-men became men.

The stage at which men habitually fashioned a diversity of artifacts for the first time is the greatest moment in the long history of technology. The forms produced probably consisted of a single component. The reason for this inference is that naturefacts are discrete physical masses, such as sticks and stones, and that such hand-held natural objects in all likelihood were transformed into artifacts simply by reducing their size in a meaningful manner. Raw material reduction was the most important processing method in the production of subsistants by foragers. Thus, a stick might be sharpened at one end or a stone reduced in size by removing flakes. Another major step was to join two or more processed components, with different inherent qualities, in order to produce a single artifact. To attach a piece of flaked stone to the end of a wooden shaft is an example. The result was an artifact with an effectiveness superior to that of either component part when used alone. Of greater technological significance, however, is the fact that this stone-pointed spear was made of two components. This joining of forms with vastly different qualities, the conjunctive process, led to momentous changes in technologies. Repeated use of such a two-unit spear would render it largely ineffective because of the "wobble factor"; the spearpoint would work its way apart from the wooden shaft. The solution was to attach the point with a binding material which was flexible and therefore would be more pliable than the shaft or point materials. The joiner may have been a lump of asphaltum or resin or a strip of sinew, skin, or vine. In any event, we now have a spear with three separate components; it is technologically more complex and functionally more effective because the third component has been added. The critical question is: Could the attachment material have been conceived as essential at the time a spear with a separate point was originally created? Given the manner in which technological innovations seem to accrete, it is difficult to conceptualize how a solution to the "problem" of a binder could have arisen before the "need" had become apparent. In terms of the components forming spears, ethnographic writings are at least tangentially significant. We find that spears made from a simple shaft of wood are rather uncommon among foragers around the world; spears with only a weapon shaft and a point are very seldom reported. Spears composed of a wooden shaft, a point made from stone or some other material, and a point-shaft binder are the norm.

In the elementary development of subsistants, and similarly of non-subsistants, one-component forms often were archetypes, to which other components were added in order to achieve superior technological efficiency. Examples follow:

skin container + sinew stitching
retrieving pole + end hook + pole-hook binder
wooden club + impaling spike + club-spike binder
stone knife blade + handle + blade-handle binder
stone adz blade + wooden handle + blade-handle binder

Although these items have no more than three components, they illustrate the principle involved in increasing the complexity of an artifact by joining more and more components. The evaluation of naturefact and artifact complexity which follows is based on the proposition that, *in general, the addition of configurationally distinct items or components indicates an increase in technological complexity.* (It also is possible that component numbers may decrease in the production of a form. This is likely to occur with the discovery of a superior raw material or one with differing properties from that used formerly. In the manufacture of a metal-pointed spear, a hollow tang might be fashioned at the base of the spearhead and the need for a point-shaft binder thereby negated. Such a change to fewer components is accommodated in the concept of a quantum leap.) The reader may be willing to admit that the previous examples illustrate reasonable steps toward increasing complexity but may ask whether, with the exception of quantum leaps, larger component numbers always indicate increased complexity. The answer is "yes" for implements, and "yes" for facilities provided it is recalled that the components of facilities must be functionally distinct to be considered as separate entities.

In terms of changes in the production of wooden spears made from a single component the following sequence is visualized as one possibility.

I   natural shaft-stick spear

II   shaft-stick spear sharpened to a point at one end

III   shaft-stick spear pointed and with a single barb

IV   shaft-stick spear pointed with multiple barbs

We see here that steps II through IV are examples of technological amplifications, or refinements in working a particular medium, wood, for a particular attribute, the point. We presume that these and other refinements in any particular medium occurred before there were quantum leaps. The latter are illustrated by each of the changes in the following sequence.

I   shaft + barbed bone point + shaft-point binder

II   shaft + barbed bone point + shaft end binder + point-shaft attachment line

III   shaft + barbed bone point + shaft end binder + wooden float + point-float attachment line

In this particular form the new components are added one at a time, but this need not always be the case. The leister (fish spear) will illustrate the process of adding duplicative components simultaneously.

   I   shaft + bone point with a single barb + shaft-point binder

   II   shaft + multi-barbed bone point + shaft-point binder

   III   shaft + 2 multi-barbed bone points + shaft-point binder

   IV   shaft + 4 multi-barbed bone points + shaft-point binder

Step I to II is a technological amplification, while step III is design amplification. Once the idea of multiple points had been introduced, it became immediately possible to expand abruptly from two to four or ten prongs. In other words, once the principle of multiplicity in a spear component had been realized, it could lead to the production of new forms which were varieties more often than types; even when the type distinction prevailed, the qualitative differences were relatively minor.

It might be asked whether the three-component spear form might not have diffused to a people, making it possible for them to bypass the simpler steps. The answer is "yes," but the fact is immaterial in terms of the general evolution of the spear. Someone, somewhere, at some previous time, must have carried out the preceding steps, and this is the only important factor in the present context.

When considering the complexity of those forms classed as facilities, the component numbers must be determined carefully on the basis of whether they are functionally differentiated parts or multiple parts, the latter being a simpler concept. For example, a hundred stones might be taken from the edge of a stream to make a dam for confining fish. Similarly, fifty bushes might be uprooted and placed in converging lines leading to a concealed hunter. In both instances the operational size of the dam or game guide will be determined by the availability of materials, the technology of the makers, the terrain, the species to be taken, the weaponry to be employed, and the number of persons involved in the operation. The number of component stones or bushes is *not* in itself significant; the important point is that a particular material is employed in a specific manner to achieve a particular end. In such instances the material utilized is recorded by name, and after the component's listing a superimposed "x" is introduced to stand for a variable numerical value. Thus, the dam is listed as 1 item: stones^x, and the game guide as 1 item: brush^x.

This taxonomy enables one to perform two different operations in the study of material culture. One is to plot the logical development of technological forms from simple to complex. This may be achieved by analyzing the manufactures made by hunters at the time of their historic contact. It is theoretically possible to compare these results with paleoethnographic recoveries for even more complete knowledge about actual sequences of development. The taxonomy has a second equally important function: by using the data to compare the manufactures in one aboriginal society with those in another, the relative complexity of subsistant inventories of different peoples may be established. However, before either step may be taken, it is essential to set forth certain guidelines and rules which must be followed when classifying forms and judging their comparative complexity.

GUIDELINES FOR UTILIZING THE TAXONOMY

Now that the major characteristics of the taxonomy have been presented, it is time to explain the steps to be followed when classifying a form and to reemphasize some of the distinctions made previously. After studying the next few pages of text, one should be able to isolate subsistants, assess the complexity of each form, and after setting aside the extraneous information, fit any particular type into the taxonomy. As is true of any classification, it is essential to learn the guidelines and rules thoroughly before attempting to apply them to an inventory of forms.

Is it a subsistant? A form is a subsistant if it is used *directly* in the procurement of food; in other words, it is manipulated, built, or triggered for the sole purpose of obtaining sustenance. The forms most commonly found among foragers around the world are the following: digging, prying, and dislodging sticks; missile sticks and clubs; hand-held or hurled spears, which may or may not be propelled with the aid of a throwing-board; harpoon darts and toggle-headed harpoons; leisters; bows and arrows; all forms of snares and traps, poisons, hooks, and nets; lures, disguises, guides, blinds, and surrounds used in food-getting purposes.

Is it a naturefact or an artifact? The naturefact-artifact distinction is based on whether or not the form is modified by man before it is used. If it is not changed in physical form before use, it is a naturefact; if it has been altered in any way, it belongs to the artifact subphylum. All forms made and used are artifacts; all forms used, but not made, are naturefacts.

Is it an aid? Any form, or technique, which is used directly as part of a method of food-getting is an aid; these occur in three distinct clusters designated as anatomical, natural, or artifactual. Anatomical aids utilize human morphology and physiology for a particular procedure; examples are whistling or calling to attract an animal or using one's hands for retrieval of plants or animals. Among natural aids, the use of fire or dogs to drive game is most common. Artifactual aids often are convey-ances: a raft used to approach waterfowl, an outrigger canoe employed in setting and tending a turtle net, a kayak to carry a man to a lead in sea ice frequented by seals. Other artifactual usages include a rope to lower a man over a cliff in order that he may take birds from their nests, or an ice pick employed to cut a hole in ice for fishing. In each instance an aid contributes to and is a part of the technique being used to obtain food.

Is it an implement or a facility? The distinction between classes depends on whether the application of human energy in the performance of a task is direct or indirect. Implements require direct energy output during their use, whereas facilities do not. All implements are handled, in the manner of a spear or a digging stick, when in use. Facilities func-tion by attracting (as in the case of a fish lure), containing (pitfall), holding (game net, fish net, or trap), restraining (gorge or fish hook), or redirecting (game guides, dams and weirs).

Is it an instrument or a weapon? If an implement is used to obtain an edible mass which is not capable, in any realistic terms, of moving away, it belongs to the subclass of instruments. Ants or termites in their nests, caterpillars in trees, shellfish, fruits, berries, nuts, roots, or tubers all may be obtained with the aid of instruments. On rare occasions instru-ments may be employed against creatures *normally* capable of significant motion; for example, a bear may be held with an instrument when it is groggy after just having come out of hibernation. Weapons, the other subclass, are used against organic masses capable of escaping in realistic terms; these are various forms of what normally are considered game animals, birds, and at times fish. Weapons are designed to injure or kill directly, and examples include spears, bows and arrows, harpoons, boomerangs, missile sticks, and rocks hurled by hand or from slings.

Is it simple or complex? The simple-complex distinction is made on the basis of the movement of parts when the subsistant is being employed. If a simple form is composed of more than one part, the parts do not change their position relative to each other during use. This may be seen in the case of an adz, a barbed leister, a hook-ended pole, or a game guide made from trees and brush. If a part merely moves onto itself, as in the case of some tether snares, the subsistant is classed as simple. Complex subsistants, on the other hand, have parts which change in their physical relationship to each other every time they come into play. Examples of complex manufactures include the bow and arrow, in which the bow string moves, as does the bow shaft, as an arrow is propelled; a deadfall, in which an animal releases a trigger, which causes a weight to crash downward; a spear which, if used with a throwing-board, moves in relationship to it; a pitfall in which the covering gives way under the weight of an animal, and so on.

Is there ever an overlap in usage which may affect classification? The answer is yes. A digging stick might be employed to dig an animal out of its burrow and kill it, as well as to dig roots; a stick might be used mainly as a missile to throw at animals but also to dig roots; an ax might be used mainly as a production tool, but also serve to dig up clams. In these and all other instances of varying uses, the alternatives are noted in parentheses after a form's description, but classification is on the basis of the principal subsistant function.

FURTHER CRITERIA DISTINCTIONS

The guidelines should enable one to identify any subsistant or aid and place it in a particular unit of the taxonomy. The distinctions to follow deal primarily with assessing the complexity of any form, that is, deciding which factors are significant and so on. Some of the decisions which follow are clearly arbitrary and might have been conceived differently. What is more important, however, is that such judgments must be made in a consistent manner.

1. *Are there any physical characteristics of subsistants which are not relevant to the taxonomy?* The answer is yes.

A. Designs or decorative elements are not considered in the analysis. The reason is that adornments do not contribute to the purpose for which a form was made. Designs painted on a spear with blood, red ocher applied to a bow, or a charm attached to a fish net did not increase the effectiveness of the form. Despite the fact that the user of such forms might have thought that decorations increased its utility, in fact they did not. The major variables involved were the subsistant's technological potential, the user's skills, and chance.

B. When establishing the number of components which comprise a subsistant, any abrasives, lubricants, or other materials used only during the manufacturing process or in the repair of forms are not considered. Thus, the emphasis is on the components of the product as a completed form.

C. The elements of a single material which go together to function as a binder are considered as one unit. Thus, a spearpoint might have been joined to a shaft with a length of rawhide thong, a lump of plant resin, two-strand twisted grass, or braided sinew. In each instance the binder is judged as a single component. If, however, rawhide and resin were used in conjunction with one another they would be considered as separate binders.

D. Alternative materials are not considered. A bow might be made from spruce or occasionally from birch, but only the fact that it was made from wood is considered significant.

2. *How may the component numbers be established?*

A. For implements, each configurationally distinct part is counted, and they are totalled.

B. Facility components which are multiples of each other or those which serve the same function are considered as one unit composed of an indefinite number of physically similar parts. Thus, if a fish weir were built of approximately 200 stones, 100 poles, and 300 tree branches, it would be recorded as stones^x, poles^x, branches^x, to represent the three components with indefinite numbers of parts in each. In the same context, if structurally similar components, poles for example, served different functions, as in use to form the sides, floor, and top of a deadfall, they would be considered as three separate units, that is, side poles^x, floor poles^x, and top poles^x.

3. *What do you do when separate forms are used together to perform a particular subsistant task?* If the objects must be combined in order to function, the component numbers are added, and they are listed as a single unit. Bow and arrow components would be totalled, as is true also of the throwing-board and the spear made for use with it. Two objects always used together are considered as *functionally linked* or simply as linked if they are from the *same taxonomic order*, such as a fish trap or a game guide and a net. However, if types are not from the same taxonomic categories, but are used together, they are *functionally related* and are listed separately; this would be the case with a leister used at a fish dam

or a spear employed to kill an animal in a pitfall. The combined usages in these instances are in terms of separate units functioning as an *association*.

4. *What about an aid serving as a part of an artifact?* It is considered together with the form involved since they are functionally linked. A dead squirrel used to bait a deadfall is a deadfall component; a live moth tied to a branch as an aid in luring an emu is regarded similarly. Without them there would be no functioning subsistant.

5. *What do you do when a number of varieties serve the same general subsistant purpose?* It might be determined that a people used three different forms of arrows: one with four components, another with six, and a third with eight. The arrow with the eight-component total is the only one classified because it represents the form with the greatest number of parts. In the tables only the form with the greatest number of components is listed. Furthermore, the total components of a type are based always on the most elaborate variety. The idea of a *unit type* means that all varieties of a type are classified in terms of the form with the greatest number of parts.

6. *What do you do when an ethnographic report is incomplete in the description of components for a form?* Components which obviously were present but are not mentioned are added, with the letter "A" for "assumed" in parentheses following the entry. If a subsistant is mentioned but not described, it may be entered and assigned the number of components which seem reasonable in terms of its reported form known elsewhere. In this instance the letters "AA" for "all assumed" are placed in parentheses after the subsistant listing. Sometimes, too, a trade item is included in a subsistant inventory, and it is distinguished from local manufactures by a "T" for "trade" in parentheses. It hardly need be added that ethnographic accounts which often require assumptions about component numbers should be avoided if at all possible.

The best test of the subsistant taxonomy just presented is to apply it to the assemblages employed by particular peoples, and this will be undertaken in the next part of the text. Such an examination should make apparent the usefulness of the units, and the merits as well as the demerits of the component analysis should be revealed. Since the guidelines and rules just presented do not deal with the minor problems which may arise when classifying forms, any elaboration necessary on a particular point is offered in a fitting context. When reading the next four chapters, which deal with the subsistants of diverse hunters, it might be helpful to keep in mind a number of questions about the classification. The first query might be whether the concept of subsistant is so restrictive that it cannot justly reflect the core of manufactures necessary for survival among gatherers. One might ask too whether or not the naturefact-artifact distinction is more cumbersome than useful in considering the nature of the technological forms considered; might this distinction be omitted? It is equally desirable to question the validity of the implement-facility dichotomy as well as the "fit" of any form into these and all of the other smaller units in the classification. A broader question is what, if anything, may be learned about the evolution of technology from the information presented? Each of these issues is raised at this point because they will be discussed at length in the closing chapters. To be aware of them now should enable the reader to consider more critically the complexity of technology in its logical evolution.

Part TWO
The Peoples

THREE

Desert Area Peoples

Among the hottest and driest areas of the habitable world are the deserts of central Australia, southern Africa, and northwestern Mexico. Some sectors of these regions had no water supplies, and their human occupants were no more than transient. Other localities, with temporary or permanent sources of water, were inhabited by small bands of peoples who lived by their skills as foragers. In this chapter and all others in which the subsistants of aborigines are described, societies have been chosen to represent man's adaptations to major climatic zones. It has been reasoned that by discussing the subsistants of hunters who lived in broadly similar environments but at a considerable distance from one another, we may come to understand what the words "ecological adaptation" mean in rather exacting contexts. Peoples were selected on the basis of two criteria above all others: they must have been separated from one another by at least 400 miles in order to negate for the most part the possibility of meaningful contacts between them, and the ethnographic information about their aboriginal lifeway must be adequate for analysis. The foragers chosen to represent central Australia are the Arunta; the Naron Bushmen will typify southern Africa, and the Seri northwestern Mexico. These peoples were so distant from one another that even the most imaginative diffusionist could not reasonably suggest that their ancestors had any direct contact during at least the past 30,000 years. Thus, independently of each other they learned to maintain themselves in stark desert habitats.

ANGMAGSALIK ESKIMOS●

●NABESNA   ●CARIBOU ESKIMOS

●OWENS VALLEY PAIUTE

●SERI

●YAHGAN

ARUNTA

The aboriginal foragers of Australia were contacted by Europeans in comparatively recent times and were found to have retained an archaic way of life into modern times more than any other major block of humanity. The first aboriginal settlers probably arrived over 30,000 years ago via a partial land bridge from the mainland of southeast Asia. Aboriginal Australians are best known for their paintings and engravings on rock faces, seemingly complex social organization, elaborate initiation ceremonies, and involved rituals designed to perpetuate the offerings of nature. Their homes are best regarded as impermanent shelters, and they built no temples for the living or elaborate graves for the dead. The breadth of their cultural achievements was limited in comparison to that of most other peoples throughout the world. Their only domestic animal was the dingo, and their manufactures not only were few, but were limited in diversity. Over most of the subcontinent they were forced by the absence of more suitable lithic materials to make their stone tools from quartz or quartzite. They did not work metals and very rarely made pottery. Since Australia supported primarily marsupial animals, the people were without horn, antler, or tusks as possible raw materials from which to fashion implements. None of the local animals other than the dingo had any potential for domestication, but neither did they prey on men (Mulvaney 1966:84–93).

In terms of landmass Australia is relatively flat with only seven percent of the country rising more than 2000 feet in elevation. Vast expanses are arid, with less than ten inches of precipitation a year, and one geographical region blends into the next to produce broad similarities of fauna and flora across the subcontinent's length and breadth. When the first British settlers arrived in 1788, Australia was occupied by about 300,000 persons, grouped into about 500 tribes with an average of 500–600 individuals per tribe (Elkin 1964:12).

Some aboriginal Australians have been well described in ethnographic accounts, and included among these are the Arunta (Aranda). They lived in and around the Macdonnell Ranges and numbered about 2000 when they were studied most intensively near the turn of the century by Walter Baldwin Spencer and Frank J. Gillen (1927). The ethnography of Spencer and Gillen is quite comprehensive, and it has been supplemented with important observations by E. C. Stirling (1896). The tribe was divided into local totemic bands; one such group, the witchetty grubs, numbered forty persons and occupied about 100 square miles of country in the vicinity of Alice Springs. Within a band one or two families wandered together from one favored locality to the next most of the year in search of food, and each band had a central gathering place where the members met to hold their most sacred ceremonies.

In their normal daily routine the men took their throwing-boards, spears, boomerangs, and shields and ranged out from their camp in search of large game. Their favored method of hunting was to conceal themselves either near water holes or along game trails. In either instance the hunters waited and speared the species which appeared. Among the mammals taken were the eruo and rock wallaby, both of which are kangaroo species, as well as the great red kangaroo. The most important bird killed was the emu, an ostrich-like bird native to Australia. Game also was ambushed in cooperative hunts; grass set afire forced the animals toward a spot where hunters were concealed. Another hunting method was to run animals down with the aid of dingoes. During an ordinary day the men hunted at some distance from camp, and the women, accompanied by their children, searched the locality for small game to capture and edible plant products to procure with digging sticks. The harvest was carried home in *pitchis* or trough-like containers. These people seemingly consumed everything edible, including snakes, frogs, flies of certain species, honey ants, and clay from anthills; however, food taboos restricted the diet of each individual to a greater or lesser degree. Normally they searched for food each day, although a surplus from one day might lead to a respite during the next day or two; foods were stored purposefully only in preparation for a ceremony.

Arunta clothing was practically nonexistent in spite of the fact that the temperature might drop to freezing at night. The men wore only pubic tassels; most women went naked, although some of them wore small pubic aprons. The absences which might be unexpected include the bow and arrow, pottery, and anything sewn.

ARTIFACTS

Instruments. By far the most versatile instrument was the digging stick made from a wooden shaft sharpened either at one or both ends. It was associated intimately with the collecting activities of women and served to remove roots, tubers, grubs, and burrowing animals from the ground. Considering the major contributions of women in the food-getting activities of aboriginal Australians, digging sticks probably reaped greater day-to-day harvests than any other form. The simplicity of using digging sticks and their productiveness cannot be emphasized enough when considering the economies of many gatherers.

Axes were used to cut chips of wood out of the trunks of trees to provide toeholds for climbing. After a man had reached the uppermost trunk or branches of a tree, he cut into the wood in search of animals, eggs, or honey. In order to obtain edible larva of a particular insect, certain species of eucalyptus trees were chopped down with axes. The stone blade for an ax was chipped and then ground to a sharp edge. It was attached (hafted) by bending the midsection of a piece of wood around the blade and tying the bent section in place with a piece of string; the blade was held firm with a mass of plant resin placed between it and the handle loop (Fig. 3–1f). Tools are designed primarily to process materials and seldom are capable of serving as subsistants; yet here is a clear example of a tool which also served as an instrument.

Weapons. Three weapon types were made by reducing the size of a piece of wood to create a one-component form. Each is regarded as a very elementary form. One was the shaft spear, which was sharpened to a point at one end and was launched by hand. Among the Arunta it was not a common form of spear, but elsewhere in Australia, especially in the north, it appears to have been a more important type (Basedow 1925:190). In technological terms it is fascinating to consider some of the variability found in Australian spears made from one piece of wood. The worked end might be barbed on one side, barbed on both sides, bifurcated, or bifurcated and barbed. These varieties were made on Melville and Bathurst islands (Spencer 1914:360–365) and appear to have been used against game as well as against men. In general terms it is remarkable that the most basic type of artifactual spear, a shaft of wood pointed at one end, existed among any peoples at the time of historic contact. This is an ancient type, but because of its sound basic utility it seemingly persisted for a vast span of time.

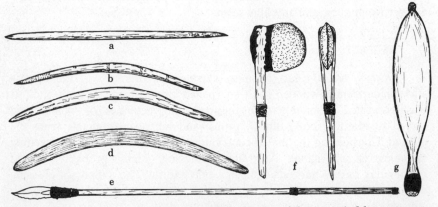

Figure 3–1.   Arunta subsistants: *a* and *b* missile sticks, *c* and *d* boomerangs, *e* stone-pointed spear, *f* ax, *g* throwing-board.

Another one-component weapon used by the Arunta was the missile stick (Fig. 3–1a, b), sometimes called a "throwing stick." These were straight or slightly curved sticks, round in cross section if straight or oval in section if they were slightly curved; seemingly the type grades into the boomerang (Stirling 1896:92–93). Missile sticks are poorly described for the Arunta, but for the Lake Eyre area people to the southeast the form is reported in considerable variety, ranging from ordinary sticks to those with spatulate or lanceolate points. It appears that they were hand held as fighting weapons, thrown in such a manner that they cartwheeled through the air, or else skipped along the ground (Horne and Aiston 1924:69–71). The digging sticks and missile sticks seem to be closely related types, with one used by women and the other by men.

The boomerang was used but was not regarded as a very effective weapon. The Arunta varieties differed somewhat in their form (Fig. 3–1c, d), but each planed as it twisted through the air to strike small game, birds, or men. There were a number of varieties manufactured by the Arunta, one of which was designed only for use in fighting. Yet the basic type was not elaborated further among these or other foragers.

A special spear for taking fish is mentioned but not described by Stirling (1896:52), nor is it clearly isolated as a type by Spencer and Gillen (1927:vol. 2, 521–525). Thus I have reconstructed the component number based on the general template for most Arunta weapons. Henceforth in this text any spear used primarily against fish will be termed a "leister." A dictionary defines a leister as a spear with three or more barbed prongs for taking fish (*Webster's Third New International Dictionary* 1961:1292); however, in this text the word will mean any spearlike weapon employed directly against fish, regardless of the number of piercing points or whether they are barbed. The dictionary definition is not realistic in terms of the technologies of foragers, since one- and especially two-pointed leisters are rather common. The term "spear" by contrast will be used with reference to simple thrust or thrown weapons employed directly against animals.

If a spear was held and then thrust or thrown by hand and if it did not change its appearance during the process, the form is termed "simple." However, when something more than human muscle power was brought into play to propel a weapon, the form is designated as "complex"; a change in its structural unity accompanies the use of this extrasomatic mechanical energy. The Arunta used a device to launch most forms of spears which utilized such a mechanical process. The manufacture has been called a throwing-board, throwing stick, spear-thrower, or atlatl, depending in most cases on the ethnographer's preference. In this book it will be called a throwing-board regardless of the terminology used in

Table 3–1   Arunta subsistants and their components.

Artifact
  implement
    instrument
      simple
        1 component
          digging stick
        4 component
          ax for food retrieval (tool): flaked & ground stone blade + wood handle + string handle binder + resin handle-blade binder
    weapon
      simple
        1 component
          shaft spear
          missile stick
          boomerang
        4 component
          leister: wood shaft + wood point + resin shaft-point binder + sinew shaft-point lashing (AA)
      complex
        6 component
          throwing-board (knife, fire saw, tray): wood body + wood peg + sinew body-peg binder + resin body-peg binder + quartzite knife blade + resin blade-body binder
        9 component
          spear: wood foreshaft + stone point + resin foreshaft-point binder + sinew foreshaft-point binder + reed shaft + resin foreshaft-shaft binder + sinew foreshaft-shaft binder + string binder at shaft base + fiber plug at shaft base
  facility
    tended set
      simple
        1 component
          blind for hunting: stones^x
        3 component
          emu guide & poison: brush^x guide fence + mud^x (A) dam & crushed poisonous leaves^x
          emu lure: head + neck + attachments (AA)
    untended set
      complex
        3 component
          emu pitfall: pit^x + brush^x cover + earth^x topping

Explanatory Note about Tables of Subsistants

In all of the tables in which the subsistants of specific peoples are presented, a parallel format is followed. In any category the least complex unit is listed first. If a people used subsistant naturefacts, these forms are presented at the head of the table. In Table 3–1 the subphylum "Artifact" appears as the most all-encompassing unit. The "implement" and "facility" classes are particular reports. A throwing-board served to "lengthen" the arm of the user and thereby enabled him to propel the spear with greater thrust. A typical form is a relatively narrow strip of wood about two feet in length with a groove or depression along the top which serves to cradle the spear. At one end is a small wooden peg, attached with resin and sinew (tendon) binding, to receive the hollowed-out end of a spear shaft (Fig. 3–1g). The opposite end of the throwing-board is surrounded by the fingers to balance the shaft until it is thrown (Fig. 3–2). At this end a stone blade mounted in resin served as a knife; the concave body might be used as a receptacle, and either of the sharp lateral edges could function as a fire-making saw. In terms of complex weapon types the combination of a throwing-board and spear is the most direct and obvious development from a simple form of weapon. Throwing-boards were used in diverse hunting societies around the world, but nowhere was the form more fully developed to serve not only its basic function but other highly varied purposes than among the Arunta and nearby peoples.

The simple shaft spear was always hand hurled, and the same appears to have been true of the leister. However, most other spears were thrown with the aid of a throwing-board. Such spears had from four to nine separate components, but only the nine-component form is included in Table 3–1. Because of its maximum component number, it represents the unit type. This form had a chipped stone point joined to a long wooden foreshaft with plant resin and sinew (Fig. 3–1e). At the base of the long foreshaft a short reed shaft was attached with resin and sinew. At the lower end of the reed a length of string was wound in order to prevent the reed from splitting, and finally a small plug of fibrous material was inserted into the base of the reed to receive the throwing-board peg. The throwing-board has six components, and together with this spear form having nine components, the functionally linked subsistant has a total of fifteen items. In Table 3–1, and all others, a dotted line indicates the functional linkage of two items forming one subsistant.

---

indented beneath the artifact subphylum because they are divisions within it. Implements, being less complex than facilities, are listed first. Within the implement class are "instruments" and "weapons" as subclasses. Since instruments are judged as the simpler of the two, they precede weapons in the table. The same is true of "tended" and "untended sets" among facilities. At the order level all forms are categorized as "simple" or "complex," with the simpler forms listed first. Within the orders the forms are listed according to their component numbers, with those having the fewest components listed first. Thus, the forms which appear at the top of the table are technologically less elaborate than those which occur lower on the page, and following the table from top to bottom presents an overall increase in complexity.

It will be noted that the ax was used not only to obtain food but as a tool; any such nonsubsistant usage is noted in parentheses. The letters "AA" follow any description in which all the components must be assumed. The throwing-board and spear are separate physical objects but function as a single subsistant and thus are joined by dotted lines. The letter "T" indicates an item acquired by trade.

Figure 3–2. Arunta hurling a spear with the aid of a throwing-board (Courtesy of the American Museum of Natural History).

In the component approach to the analysis of subsistants one nagging point must be raised, and this is as appropriate a time to do so as any other. It has been reasoned that the components making up a subsistant type (with due consideration to the rules and guidelines in Chapter 2) were all essential. In other words, there were no parts which did not contribute meaningfully to the whole. Thus on technological grounds we might expect a spear to consist of a point + a shaft + a point-shaft binder. Yet in the most elaborate Arunta spear we have a tripling of this number; the question is why? Could it be from technological custom without a rational basis, or were all the parts necessary as a result of the qualities of the raw materials used, the game hunted, the hunting techniques, or the terrain over which the weapons were used? We do not really know because the ethnographic descriptions do not include Arunta thoughts about their weapons nor is specific information available about spear usages. A number of observations seem appropriate. The different spear forms probably served different purposes or functions, but this cannot be proven from data available. The component total is in part large because of the practice of binding spear joints both with resin and sinew. It is tempting to infer that these materials were combined because neither was in itself satisfactory. And yet if this were the case, why did so many other peoples around the world use only one of these binders on a weapon point? Possibly convention rather than a sound technological basis guided the Arunta usage in their spearpoint binders. This seems particularly reasonable when it is noted that the knife blade at the base of a throwing-board, which probably received more abrupt and forceful blows than any resin-sinew joint, was attached only with resin and the separate barb on one wooden spearpoint was attached only with sinew. Thus the combination of resin and sinew as a binder may be technologically redundant, leading to component totals which falsely represent the technological complexity of the item. If this is true, as is suspected in certain instances, then we are confronted with at least a certain amount of "noise" in the complexity measure.

Facilities. The division of facilities into the subclasses of tended and untended sets has been drawn in order to distinguish between forms which required the presence of man in order to function (tended) and those which operated in man's physical absence (untended). Each of the three tended sets of the Arunta was employed to make prey more vulnerable for the effective employment of weaponry. The great utility of such forms is appreciated when it is realized that an Arunta spear hurled with a throwing-board had a very short range. Spencer and Gillen (1927: vol. 1, 16) wrote that "it takes an exceptionally good man to kill or disable at more than twenty yards," while Stirling (1896:88) wrote that the accuracy range for this weapon was not more than fifty yards. Along the coast of eastern Australia, James Cook (Beaglehole 1955:vol. 1, 396) reported that the form was accurate at a distance of forty to fifty yards. The limited effective range of a spear, along with the arid nature of the Arunta habitat, makes it understandable that much of their hunting focused at water holes. One technique was to build a blind of stones or brush near water in order to conceal a hunter. Another more involved technique was to build a brush fence leading to a dammed off section of a water hole in which the crushed leaves of a poisonous plant had been placed. When an emu drank the water, it lost its sense of balance and could be killed readily. One brief reference is made to an emu hunting lure which is described as "something which resembles the long neck and small head of the bird" (Spencer and Gillen 1927:vol. 1, 16). A hunter used the lure as he approached an emu, which drew nearer out of curiosity. When the bird was within a short distance, the hunter launched his spear. There is no indication of how many components the lure had, and I arbitrarily have assigned it three: the head, neck, and attachments. At localities where emu were known to feed, one form of untended set was utilized. A pit was dug, and at the bottom of it a spear was placed with the point facing upward. On top of the pit brush was spread, and it was covered with earth. An emu walking over the trap fell through and was transfixed by the spear. In this instance, since spears belong to a different taxonomic order than the pitfall, their combined use is considered as an association. In general we would expect that the greater the use of untended sets over tended sets, the more developed the hunting technology. It often has been asserted that aboriginal Australians represent an archaic way of life, and this would seem to be true with reference to the frequency of game sets among them. On a continent-wide basis tended sets were relatively common, while very few types of untended sets were known. The most important of the untended forms was the pitfall.

AIDS

One of the best-known natural aids employed by Australian hunters was the dingo (*Canis dingo*), and it was utilized by the Arunta. How long man and the dingo had been associated in Australia is not known, but one estimate is at least 3000 to 4000 years. At the time of historic contact the dingo was distributed over the entire continent, but it was less common in the wetter regions. It appears that dingoes are best considered as quasi-domestic animals since they most often appear to have been captured as pups and raised by the aborigines. In the one comprehensive study by M. J. Meggitt (1965) it was concluded that the dingo was not a very effective hunting aid. The Arunta sometimes ran down game with the help of dingoes, but it appears to have been more common for men to drive game into ambush by themselves or by setting fire to grasslands. After an area had been burned over, burrowing species were retrieved with the aid of digging sticks. Anatomical aids, because they seem so obvious, often are ignored or badly slighted in ethnographic reports. We know that the Arunta collected the eggs of emu and other birds, while frogs, crayfish, certain insects, berries, fruits and seeds were eaten, presumably after being obtained by hand. One fishing technique was for men to form a line across a water hole and frighten the fish to one end, from which they were taken with leisters.

Associations. All of the subsistant unit types identified among the Arunta are recorded in Table 3–1. The Arunta used two instruments, five weapons, and four facilities, making a total of eleven subsistant types. These forms were employed with aids in the following associations:

poisoned water hole: poison/ dam for poison/ brush fence guide/ spear & throwing-board
game drive # 1: dingo/ spear & throwing-board
game drive # 2: fire/ spear & throwing-board (digging stick)
lure: emu lure/ spear & throwing-board
blind: emu blind/ spear & throwing-board
pitfall: emu pitfall/ fixed spear in pit

The most notable characteristics of these associations are that most of the specialized hunting techniques were for emu and that spears are a part of each one.

Since Arunta subsistants are the only ones described thus far, it would be unwise to attempt any broad generalizations, but one comment is appropriate. Aboriginal Australians are renowned in ethnographic literature for the "poverty" of their material culture and its "simplicity." Whether the eleven subsistants of the Arunta will verify this judgment remains to be seen.

NARON BUSHMEN

The Bushmen probably occupied much of southern Africa at the time the European colonization began, but for hundreds of years thereafter they were massacred by colonists as well as by the Hottentots and Bantu-speaking Africans (Tobias 1964:70). In modern times they have survived mainly in the extremely isolated and arid areas of South West Africa and in Bechuanaland. It was thought that the Bushmen had become nearly extinct, but in 1964, Richard B. Lee (1966 12:21) determined that their population was about 44,000. Of this number about 10,000 Bushmen still followed a foraging way of life. While considerable ethnographic information is available about the Bushmen as they live today, no entirely satisfactory account exists about their techno-economic life as it functioned before the effects of European contacts. With some misgivings but little alternative, I have chosen to concentrate on the Naron group, who lived in South West Africa and were studied over a six-month period in 1921–1922 by Dorothea F. Bleek (1928). These data are supplemented with information collected by Richard B. Lee (1966) in 1963–1964 among the Kung Bushmen who lived along the Bechuanaland and South West African border. Bleek was most interested in the Naron language, but she also recorded in brief a broad range of ethnographic information. At that time European-Naron contacts apparently had not led to any radical change in the lives of these Bushmen, but game laws were being enforced with enough effectiveness to force them to consume a greater proportion of vegetable foods than had been the case in aboriginal times. The Naron bands occupied areas surrounding water holes, and as many as twenty brush shelters formed a camp with a population up to eighty at any one time. Like the desert-dwelling Australians, rather than camp at the water holes and disturb the game that frequented them, they lived a short distance away. Their seasonal wanderings were dictated by the availability of food and water; in general, they passed the summer in one locality and wintered in another. Few details are offered concerning hunting methods, but it is noted that as a rule a man hunted alone or in the company of a boy, which suggests that cooperative hunting enterprises were uncommon if attempted at all.

ARTIFACTS

Instruments. Considering the importance of the digging stick among the Arunta, we might expect that it would occupy a similar position among the Naron. Bleek (1928:7) mentions that bulbs, tubers, and roots were obtained, but she does not cite the means, although the digging stick is mentioned specifically in the text of one myth (Bleek 1928:49). It might be that among them, as among the Kung, most plant foods consisted of nuts, berries, and melons, none of which were dug up. The Kung digging stick is described as being sharpened to a blade at one end (Lee 1966:124). Some Bushmen apart from the Naron and Kung had comparatively elaborate digging sticks. They perforated a round stone and inserted the shaft through the opening; the stone served as a weight and facilitated more effective digging. Sometimes a piece of wood was wedged between the stone and the stick to prevent the ring from slipping (Dunn 1931: 104–105; van Rippen 1918:75–79).

Another simple instrument was designed to remove or restrain hares, anteaters, and snakes. It consisted of as many as four reeds lashed end-to-end with sinew to form one long pole with a horn hook attached to one end. The hook end was shoved down an animal's hole or burrow, and its flesh was hooked so that it either could be dragged rapidly into the open and killed or could be held until another person could dig down and kill it. This particular form is considered as having nine separate parts: four are the reeds, three are their binders of sinew, and the hook and its binder complete the type. The component number of nine for this form is greater than would be anticipated for a simple instrument. The reason for the large total is that it was necessary to fit a number of reeds together in order to create a pole of sufficient length to serve effectively. The duplication of pole components closely approximates construction qualities reported for facilities. (If it were classified as a facility, the component number would be four.) However, since this game-removing hook was hand manipulated against creatures which could not effectively move or escape, it is an instrument. In a sense it might seem to be a facility, because it restrained an animal and because its component relationships are of a nature more often found among facilities. In this instance taxonomic distinctions are blurred; in defense of the taxonomy as it stands, examples of this nature tend to be infrequent.

Weapons. The only one-component, simple weapon was a missile stick, which had a rounded head and often is called a *knobkerrie* when reported in Africa. These sticks were carried by men and were used either as instruments or weapons; since the latter function appears to have been more important, the form is placed in the weapon subclass. On logical grounds we would expect that the most elementary forms of implements would serve more diverse purposes than those which were more developed, and this is precisely what is reported for the Naron missile stick. It served to dig up plant products, to club small animals to death, and to stun animals or men when thrown at them. The Naron owned a few spears, which were hand-hurled, but they were seldom used. The spearheads, which were made from metal, had been received in trade as finished products. The Kung of recent times used spears mainly to kill wounded animals; they did not serve as primary weapons of attack.

The Naron bow consisted of a simple shaft of wood (self bow) which was bound at the center and at each end with sinew. At the upper end of the bow shaft a small piece of leather attached to the sinew prevented the bow string of sinew from slipping after the bow was strung. There was only one arrow form; it was not feathered and was made from a reed shaft which had a binding of grass around the distal end. The point was fashioned from an ostrich bone sharpened at one end and rounded at the opposite end. Either end could be fitted into the grass binder. The purpose of the removable point was to reverse it when an arrow was being carried and thus protect the hunter from accidental contact with the poisoned tip. The poisoning solution was made from a beetle crushed at a particular stage in its development and a liquid mixed together. Similarly, the Kung fashioned only a single form of arrow; it too was poisoned at the tip (Lee 1966:127–128). Only one arrow type appears to have been required since the poison made it effective against diverse forms of game.

Facilities. These people did not use hunting disguises, but they did

Table 3–2   Naron Bushman subsistants and their components.

Artifact
  implement
    instrument
      simple
        1 component
            digging stick
        9 component
            game-removing hook: 4 reed poles + 3 sinew pole binders + horn
              hook + pole-hook binder
    weapon
      simple
        1 component
            missile (digging, clubbing weapon) stick
        3 component
            spear: wood shaft + metal spearpoint (T) + sinew shaft-point binder
      complex
        6 component
  ┌ ─ ─ bow: wood bow shaft + 2 sinew end bindings + sinew mid-shaft
  │   binder + leather catch at upper end of sinew binding + sinew
  │   bowstring
  │
  │ 5 component
  └ ─ ─ arrow: reed shaft + distal shaft-end grass binder + ostrich bone
            point + 2 component poison
  facility
    tended set
      simple
        1 component
            termite trap hole[x]
        3 component
            hunting blind: excavated hole[x] + earth mound[x] + green branches[x]
              on mound
    untended set
      simple
        4 component
            baited bird snare: fiber snare line + bait stick + melon + bushes as
              snare line tie[x]
      complex
        7 component
            small mammal spring pole snare: circle of upright sticks[x] + arched
              twig + snare-line holding stick + tether stick at center of depres-
              sion + grass snare-hole cover[x] + snare line + bent tree

make blinds near salt licks frequented by game animals. A man excavated
a hole near the lick, piled the earth into a mound, and on top of it stuck
green branches. Animals approaching the salt lick did not see the hunter,
which made it possible to shoot them with arrows at close range. One

tended set was used to take termites. After a rain a hole was dug into one side of the nest, exposing an underground network of passages. As the white termites attempted to leave their nest, they dropped to the bottom of the hole, from which they were scooped and processed for consumption.

Two different forms of snares were made. Since the line of the tether-snare changed only unto itself, this form is judged as "simple." The multiple components of the second type changed in their relative positions, which makes it a "complex" set; since neither required the presence of a man in order to function, they are untended sets. The simple snare was set for ostrich, bustards (paauw), and other birds. A thin stick was inserted into a small tsama melon, and one end of a line was tied to the stick. At the opposite end of the line a slipknot was made and a noose formed. The line was looped over a tree branch, with the noose hanging at one end and the melon hanging at the center of the noose; the opposite end was tied to the bushes where the set was made. A bird swallowed the melon and in the process pulled the slipknot tightly around its neck and was strangled. The complex snare was of the spring-pole variety and was set for small bucks and hares. Around the edges of a natural depression, about a foot wide and some six inches in depth, a small enclosure was formed of vertical sticks. An opening was left in one spot, and across it was placed an arched stick with a twig suspended from it. A noose fashioned in the snare line was laid on the ground around the circle of sticks. The line was hooked over a vertical stick in the center of the set and then led through the arch, where it was attached to the suspended stick, and finally on to a bent-over tree. The set was covered with grass, and when an animal moved the arched stick, the central snareline jerked loose from the tether, and the snared animal was lifted into the air by one leg. Spring-pole snares incidentally were not known in Australia, although snares attached to the end of a pole which was held by a hunter were rather common there (Anell 1960:74–75, 104).

AIDS

Near the end of the winter season, grasslands were purposefully burned in order to encourage the growth of bulb plants. This is a clear indication of planning for future subsistence welfare, which sometimes is not attributed to foragers. The use of fire in food-getting efforts is mentioned only in this context. Perhaps the Naron also followed the Kung practice of asphyxiating animals in their burrows and then retrieving them with digging sticks (Lee 1966:129). According to Bleek (1928:16) dogs were not kept by the Bushmen in aboriginal times, but the Naron owned a few dogs at the time of the study. These sometimes were used to take hares and other small game. Among the Kung studied more recently by Lee (1966:130), packs of hunting dogs were extremely important aids.

The descriptions of the Naron by Bleek are brief, and at times the technological details are unclear or even unreported. Furthermore, the text is not accompanied by meaningful illustrations of the artifacts described, which makes the reconstruction of forms even more difficult. At the same time it does appear that this work includes all of the subsistants in habitual use. A further indication of the fullness of Bleek's discussion is that it compares favorably with the Kung artifacts listed, but not discussed, by Lee (1966:122–130).

Associations. In terms of subsistant associations the following occur among the Naron:

hunting blind: blind/ bow & arrow
burrowing animal retrieval: game-removing hook/ missile stick

The Naron association total of two compared with the Arunta total of six suggests that the hunting methods of these Bushmen were less specialized and thus simpler than those identified among the Arunta. At the same time the fact that the Naron used an effective poison to tip their arrows suggests that this weapon was highly effective in an uncomplicated form. However, further comparisons among desert peoples must be withheld until the Seri have been described.

SERI

Along the northwestern coast of Mexico in the state of Sonora the Seri lived in a starkly arid setting fronting the Gulf of California. In certain respects it would seem that these people are unsuitable for discussion. Their first contacts with Europeans took place around 1540, but these were only fleeting. Effective contact did not take place until around 1700, and whites did not penetrate their major stronghold, Tiburon Island, until 1844. Of the two ethnographers who described them, W J McGee (1898) was convinced that the Seri were an extremely primitive people, and as a result of this premise some of his interpretations are clearly distorted. McGee spent only a very brief period among the Seri, and the second ethnographer, Alfred L. Kroeber, also made only a short field trip to the area. Kroeber (1931:18) made the following comment about McGee's study:

His work impresses me as that of an extraordinarily good observer, keen in seeing significant evidence, but of uncontrolled imagination and unconscious of his preconceptions. It is only fair to state that where he founds an interpretation on slender or uncertain data he generally indicates the fact to a careful reader.

The balanced nature of Kroeber's report in part offsets the biases of McGee, and yet neither man gained more than passing familiarity with the people involved. The Seri were isolated from the balance of Mexico by forbidding deserts, and they were a fiercely independent people. The distinct possibility exists that the descriptions of them represent a deculturative way of life resulting from historic persecution by other Indians and Mexicans. The Seri are nonetheless worthy of inclusion because their lifeway, although it may have been altered from aboriginal times, was viable and ongoing when described.

The Seri occupied Tiburon Island on the Gulf of California and also lived along the adjacent coast of Sonora in northwestern Mexico. Their aboriginal population possibly was about 3000, and they ranged over nearly 2000 square miles of desert country in which permanent water sources were rare. Their dwellings, which were impermanent brush shelters with bent-pole frames, were located at considerable distances from water sources. The standard garments of both sexes were a pelican-skin kilt and a short woven shirt with wide sleeves. In cold weather a pelican-skin robe was added; this robe also served as a blanket.

The most important dietary item, the green sea turtle, contributed about one-fourth of the food supply and was taken with the aid of a harpoon dart. Of equal importance as foods were fish and shellfish. The former were taken by hand at low tide after a storm or with the aid of a leister or harpoon dart, while clams were dug up at low tide with a stick or half a shell or simply by hand. The pelican was also an important food; these birds were clubbed to death in cooperative hunts conducted as the birds slept on islands at night. Mule deer were hunted with bows and arrows or were chased by several men alternately until the deer dropped from exhaustion. Hares were run down by boys. The most important plant foods were cactus fruits, mesquite beans, and a variety of seeds.

NATUREFACTS

Instruments. Although McGee was perhaps impressed unduly by the simplicity of Seri material culture, he appears to have been an accurate observer, and he reported a number of natural objects which were em-

Figure 3–3.   A Seri man wearing a kilt made from pelican skins (Courtesy of Museum of the American Indian, Heye Foundation).

ployed as simple instruments. Perhaps the most notable of these, because of the diverse purposes which it served, was the beach pebble. It appears to have been used to dig up shellfish, and it was definitely employed as a general-purpose basher, chopper, and grinder. Shellfish were dug up with sticks also or with bivalve shells. Finally, tree branches or cane shafts were used to retrieve otherwise inaccessible cactus fruits. As described, these sticks, shells, and stones served diverse and important functions in Seri subsistence activities. It should be noted that each of these forms was utilized in order to obtain food from sources incapable of movement.

ARTIFACTS

Weapons. No implement comparable to the digging stick of the Arunta or Naron was made. In terms of simple weapons a club was used to kill sleeping pelicans or exhausted deer, but it is not described and may have been an unmodified stick. The Seri made a spear, which was not described, and a two-prong leister.

One complex weapon was the self bow; strung with fiber string it propelled two different varieties of hunting arrows. The small game arrow with eight components had a blunted point. The large game arrow, the unit type, consisted essentially of a stone point fitted into a foreshaft which was joined to a shaft and was vaned with three feathers.

A harpoon unquestionably was the most important weapon employed for taking sea creatures in the Gulf of California. The harpoons used by hunters are of two basic types, depending on whether the detachable point penetrated flesh and held by the toggling principle (toggle-headed harpoon) or by the friction of the point, which often had one or more barbs on it (harpoon dart). The harpoon dart and the toggle-headed harpoon were primarily wounding and holding weapons; they often did not kill the quarry. The Seri made harpoon darts which had a long wooden shaft with a concavity at the distal end, and into this recess was fitted a barbed or an unbarbed point. In McGee's time the points were made from iron, but previously they appear to have been fashioned from sea mammal ivory. The barbless form of dart head (Fig. 3–4a) was used against sea turtles, whereas the barbed form appears to have been employed against fish and perhaps porpoises and sharks (Fig. 3–4b). The barbless harpoon dart was launched from a reed boat at a turtle, and when the weapon point struck, the foreshaft and point detached from the shaft as a unit. One end of a rope was tied to the foreshaft, and the opposite end was held by the hunter in order to play the turtle until it was drowned or driven ashore and killed, possibly with a club or stone.

AIDS

The Seri owned dogs, but they appear to have served mainly as camp scavengers, not as aids in hunting activities. Young men utilized a natural lure as a means for taking fish without the aid of subsistant artifacts or

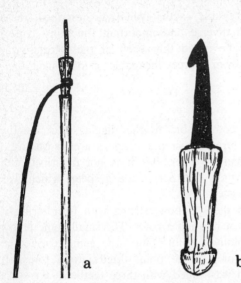

Figure 3–4. Seri subsistants: *a* barbless harpoon dart assembly, *b* barbed harpoon dart head.

Figure 3–5. A Seri man propelling a reed boat with a harpoon dart for taking sea turtles (Courtesy of Museum of the American Indian, Heye Foundation).

Table 3–3 Seri subsistants and their components.

Naturefact
  implement
    instrument
      simple
        1 component
            shell excavator (knife, paddle, cup)
            pebble shellfish remover (basher, chopper, grinder)
            shellfish digging stick
            fruit-removing stick
Artifact
  implement
    weapon
      simple
        1 component
            club for killing pelicans (deer)
        3 component
            spear: point + wood shaft + point-shaft binder (AΛ)
        4 component
            leister: 2 barbed prongs + wood shaft + points-shaft binder (A)
      complex
        2 component
            bow: wood shaft + fiber bow string

        11 component
            large game arrow: chipped-stone point + wood foreshaft + gum
                point-foreshaft binder + sinew point-foreshaft binder + cane shaft
                + sinew foreshaft-shaft binder + 3 feather vanes + sinew feather-
                shaft binder + nock-end sinew binder

---

        5 component
            harpoon dart: barbless (barbed) ivory point + wood foreshaft + gum
                point-foreshaft binder + cane shaft + foreshaft line

---

naturefacts. They tied a young or wounded pelican to one end of a rope and the opposite end to a stone. The hunter who made the stake-out hid nearby, and whenever a free pelican brought the captive a fish, the hunter took it before the pelican could swallow. Suggestively this was more a game than a serious means for obtaining food. The only artifactual aid was a reed boat constructed from three bundles of canes. The bundles were bound with mesquite root, and they were joined to each other with the same material. These vessels were propelled with a double-bladed paddle, poles, shells, or harpoon shafts.

Associations. The list of associations is limited and indicates the uncomplicated employment of subsistants.

sea hunting: harpoon dart/ reed boat
sea fishing: leister/ reed boat
pelican hunting: club/ reed boat

The most remarkable characteristic of Seri subsistant usages, apart from the simplicity and small number of forms employed, is the fact that blinds, disguises, or other forms of artifactual facilities do not appear to have been utilized. The Seri possessed no hunting or fishing subsistants which functioned in their absence, nor even any which operated as tended sets except for the practice of youths to fish with the aid of a pelican.

COMPARISONS

The definition of subsistant was conceived in order to isolate precisely the cluster of forms directly necessary for food-getting and therefore comprising the material basis for physical survival among hunters. Ethnologists often have commented on the small number and narrow range of subsistence-oriented artifacts used by foragers. Even so, I find it surprising that the Naron and Seri employed only nine types and the Arunta only eleven. If nothing else, the subsistant approach to the technologies of these foragers impressively demonstrates how few objects were essential for obtaining food.

In this and all other chapters in which the subsistants of particular peoples are discussed, a cluster of three societies has been presented. It was reasoned that a small sample for each major climatic region would be satisfactory if the ethnographic data were reasonably reliable. It might be objected that as representatives of desert life the inland inhabitants, the Arunta and Naron, should not be compared with the Seri, who lived along the seacoast in a very different type of desert setting. In terms of my goals this difference is desirable, however, since I seek to make comparisons of subsistant technologies found in grossly similar environmental zones but preferably with dissimilar floral and faunal assemblages. By comparing subsistant technologies at the order level the parameters are in terms of types or unit types, their component numbers, associations with other subsistants or aids, and the range of orders represented. In addition some comparisons pertinent only to the data for one or two of the three peoples in a chapter may be offered and conclusions drawn which are necessarily of a more limited scope.

Minimal subsistant inventory for desert foragers. On the basis of the data presented in Table 3–4, I am led to conclude that early historic gatherers could not have survived in extremely dry areas without the following forms:

2 simple instruments, one being a digging stick
2 simple weapons, one being a spear
1 complex weapon: either the bow and arrow or spear and throwing-board

Table 3–4   Arunta, Naron, and Seri subsistants compared.

	ARUNTA	NARON	SERI
Naturefact			
implement			
instrument			
simple			shell excavator
			pebble shellfish remover
			shellfish digging stick
			fruit-removing stick
Artifact			
implement			
instrument			
simple	digging stick	digging stick	
	ax	game-removing hook	
weapon			
simple	shaft spear	metal-pointed spear	spear
	missile stick		
	boomerang	missile stick	club
	leister		leister
complex	spear & throwing-board	bow & arrow	bow & arrow
			harpoon dart
facility			
tended set			
simple	blind	blind	
	game guide & poison	termite trap hole	
	emu lure		
untended set			
simple		baited bird snare	
complex	pitfall	spring-pole snare	
Type Totals	11	9	9
Component Totals	37	40	30
Associations	6	2	3

With these five items in addition to production tools and at least one carrying container, basic survival could have been achieved. Since none of these people used only instruments or only weapons in their food-getting activities, it seems reasonable to postulate that pure hunting or pure collecting economies did not exist in extreme deserts.

Subsistant complexity. The combined Arunta, Naron, and Seri type total is twenty-nine, of which nearly one-half (13 forms) had a single component. This suggests rather strongly that certain simple subsistants had a high degree of utility and possibly were types which had been used for thousands if not millions of years. The Arunta throwing-board and spear combination had the greatest number of components (15), followed by the bow and arrow of the Seri (13) and of the Naron (11). It should be noted that in spite of the fact that the Naron used poisoned arrowpoints, the component total for their bow and arrow approximates that of the Seri. At this point there are so few totals available that it is not possible to generalize effectively about the maximums. These figures do, however, make one wonder whether there is a clear upper limit to the component number for any particular type.

Associations. The range is from six for the Arunta to two for the Naron and three among the Seri. The comparatively large number for the Arunta is explained in terms of their specialized techniques for taking emu. The implication is that species-specific hunting techniques are likely to involve more forms from different orders and more aids than do techniques of a more generalized nature. We might infer that Naron and Seri hunting techniques were less developed than those of the Arunta, as indicated by less specialization in their hunting.

Overall complexity. Naron subsistants were slightly more complex than those of the Arunta since they had more components per unit type. However, this technological separation is not judged great enough to be significant. The Seri inventory is the simplest; they had the fewest forms, the smallest number of components, and no facilities.

Additional interpretations. If the Arunta and Naron subsistant totals are considered to best typify desert foragers, since no sea hunting is involved in their area, the minimal inventory would be as follows:

2 simple instruments, one of which is the digging stick
2 simple weapons, the missile stick and spear
1 complex weapon, the bow and arrow or spear and throwing-board
1 simple facility, a blind
1 complex facility

Possibly this list is more realistic than that which included the Seri inventory as minimal. In some respects it would seem justified to question the completeness of the Seri data. However, my inclination is to accept the observations of McGee as valid for the period when he was among them. I suspect that their subsistant number was greater at the time when they were first encountered during the early historic period. Persecutions by other Indians and especially by the Mexicans possibly reduced the Seri to a point at which only a minimal inventory of transportable objects was employed in order to gain a maximum degree of physical mobility. McGee (1898:13–14) noted that with the approach of strangers the Seri could disappear from a camp at a moment's notice. This would help to explain the high proportion of naturefacts among them and the absence of facilities. Whether or not the Seri were undergoing the process of deculturation, it would appear that their subsistant number approached a minimum for survival. Perhaps the most important point is that if they were able to survive with very few forms because they were badly persecuted, other foragers who faced similar conditions could have survived. If this is so, then the Seri inventory is extremely valuable.

In terms of paleoethnography one inviting question to ask is which subsistants were likely to be preserved in an open habitation site and the surrounding area after about 2000 years. For the Arunta the stone blinds might be expected to remain in their original form, and portions of three artifacts would endure: the knife blade in the throwing-board handle, the ax blade, and the stone spearpoint. For the Naron only the traded, metal spearpoint might last. The shells and stones used by the Seri would be preserved but possibly would not be identifiable as having been used by man. The only Seri artifact component likely to be preserved would be the chipped stone point used on arrows for taking large game. Thus, in the combined subsistant total of twenty-nine types, portions of seven probably would be recovered, and one other—the blind of stones—might be found complete. This is not very heartening for excavators, but the occurrence of nonsubsistants would add other dimensions to these remains. The ethnographic information about the Arunta, Naron, and Seri suggests that if weapon points were recovered from dwelling sites in a desert setting, we may then assume that the other forms in the minimal subsistant inventory were also present. How far back in time this conclusion may be projected is another issue.

FOUR

Tropical Zone Peoples

While desert settings are often judged hostile for human occupants, tropical areas are considered rich in food resources and conducive to a leisurely way of life. In fact it often is presumed that man's genesis took place in a jungle habitat and that from here he ventured into open grasslands and finally ranged far beyond both settings. One observation is clear, however; by early historic times the people in most tropical areas of the world cultivated the soil and may or may not have relied secondarily on hunting, fishing, or collecting for a living. All the Pacific islanders except those in and around Australia were farmers; cultivators also were found in most of tropical Africa, in the Americas, and in southeast Asia. Thus we must turn to the more isolated tropical settings, small islands, in order to record the ways of gatherers. The peoples selected to represent the tropical zone are the Andaman Islanders who lived adjacent to the western side of the Malay Peninsula, the Ingura on Groote Eylandt of northern Australia, and the Pitapita of northwestern Queensland in Australia. The Pitapita homeland, while a tropical habitat, bordered on a temperate zone.

ANDAMANESE

The Andaman Islands, located in the Sea of Bengal, support a dense tropical forest vegetation from which diverse roots, fruits, seeds, and honey were collected. Wild pigs and the civet cat were the only large mammals, but there were many different species of birds and some reptiles present. The frequent indentations of the coastline offered marine resources such as crustaceans, mollusks, and small fish in tidal pools; farther seaward were large fish, green and hawksbill turtles, porpoises, and dugong. The Negrito inhabitants are estimated to have numbered some 5500, and they occupied some 2500 square miles. Europeans settled permanently on the Andaman Islands in 1858 when the English established a penal colony at Port Blair. By the time the Andamanese were studied by Alfred R. Radcliffe-Brown in 1906–1908, they had become a remnant population, even though some of their groups had had relatively little contact with Europeans. Thus, the observations by Radcliffe-Brown (1948) were nearly three generations removed from the point of the earliest intensive contact, and yet because most of the people had infrequent dealings with the intruders, considerable continuity in their customs had remained. Although Radcliffe-Brown is not best known for his discussions of material culture, the appendix to his Andamanese study deals with this subject and is quite comprehensive. What is particularly important in the present context is that he was careful to distinguish between aboriginal and post-contact forms. The information which he provided may be checked in part against the observations of Edward H. Man, who was stationed on the Andaman and Nicobar islands from 1869 to 1901. Man (1882, 1883) wrote a series of articles about the Andamanese based on eleven years of living among them, and these later were published as a book. However, since he did not always distinguish between indigenous and contact-inspired forms, the ethnography of Radcliffe-Brown proved to be more useful when attempting to determine aboriginal base-line subsistants.

If we consider the Andamanese to be a single society, they may be divided into the Great and Little Andaman subgroups, each with separate and independent bands. Some bands were confined to the coast; one exploited only the interior; the majority frequented both coastal and inland forested areas. On an average there were ten linked bands per group with each band exploiting an area of approximately sixteen square miles. A band numbered forty to fifty persons, and within each were small family units consisting of a man, his wife, and their unmarried children.

The material culture to be described is for bands whose area was primarily coastal but whose members also exploited inland resources on Great Andaman Island. Each band had a favored camping site which was likely to be occupied for the longest part of the year; other camps were frequented by family groups for no more than a few months at a time. Throughout the year the people fished and collected mollusks, but during the five-month rainy season the men concentrated mainly on hunting pigs in the forests and netting turtles at sea. Man (1883:343) estimated that one-third of their food consisted of roots, fruits, and honey. The balance of their diet was composed of pigs, civet cats, iguana, turtles, fish, and mollusks, supplemented irregularly with birds.

The Andamanese lacked many cultural features which we have come to expect among hunters. They did not produce fire, own dogs, or use animal skins as materials, and their stoneworking was confined to non-subsistant productions. Among the artifacts anticipated but not present were snares or traps for game, hooks or traps for taking fish, the harpoon, and spears or missile sticks. They did, however, manufacture pottery. Naturefacts as subsistants were not represented, although they used numerous natural objects for a variety of other purposes.

ARTIFACTS

Instruments. Two simple instruments were formed from single components: the digging stick, sharpened either at one or both ends and used to obtain roots, and a pole with a natural hook at one end for taking crabs. An adz served to cut mollusks free and to remove honey from hollow trees as well as for general cutting. It consisted of a wooden handle, a shell blade, and a fiber blade-handle lashing (Fig. 4–1d). Another three-

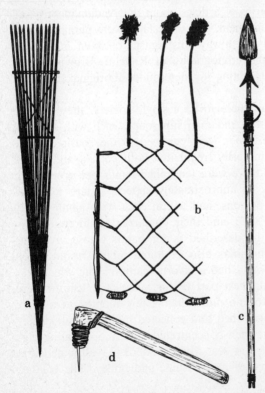

Figure 4–1. Andamanese subsistants: *a* leister, *b* turtle and fish net, *c* detachable-pointed pig arrow, *d* adz.

Figure 4–2.   An Andaman Islander shooting fish (Courtesy of the American Museum of Natural History).

component instrument was the fruit-picking hook, made by using a fiber binding to fasten a wooden hook at one end of a bamboo pole. With the use of the digging stick, adz, and fruit-picking pole, about one-third of all Andamanese food was obtained.

Weapons. The only simple weapon was a club for detaching the tail of a stingray taken by a hunter in a canoe. The self bow of the South Andamanese, a segment of the Great Andaman group, had pointed ends near which fiber strings were bound to prevent the bowstring from slipping toward the center of the bow. The fiber strings at the ends are a good example of an elaboration in the absence of nocks (notches) cut near the ends of the bow to hold the string in place. The fiber bowstring was tied to one end of the bow and looped at the opposite end so that it could be slipped into place to string the bow. Thread was bound around the attachment loop, and the bowstring was covered with beeswax, which is considered a component of the completed form; in addition, thread was bound around the bowstring to strengthen the point at which it would receive the arrow nock.

Three distinct arrow forms, none of which was feathered, were used with the bow. The fish arrow had six components, and the two other arrows were used when hunting wild pigs. The variety with a fixed point had seven components and served mainly to kill pigs which had been

Table 4–1   Andamanese subsistants and their components.

Artifact
  implement
    instrument
      simple
        1 component
            digging stick
            hook-ended crabbing stick
        3 component
            fruit-picking hook: bamboo pole + wood hook + fiber pole-hook
              binder
            adz (cutting tool, collecting instrument): wood handle + shell blade
              + fiber handle-blade binder
    weapon
      simple
        1 component
            wood club
      complex
        7 component
  ┌ – – – bow: wood body + 2 nock strings + fiber bowstring + bowstring
  │   wax + string finger grip + bowstring loop lashing
  │   ──
  │   11 component
  └ – – – detachable-pointed pig arrow: wood shaft + proximal shaft end thread
              binder + distal end thread binder + wood foreshaft + foreshaft-
              shaft cord + cord wax coat + shell point + 2 bone barbs
              + thread foreshaft-point-barb binder + barb-point-cord end binder
              waterproofing
  facility
    tended set
      simple
        4 component
            leister: wood splints^x + separation sticks^x + fiber stick-splint binder
              + fiber handle binder^x
        6 component
            dip net & poison: wood net frame hoop-handle + 2 item netting^x +
              wooden handle binder + netting-hoop binder (A) + poison
        8 component
            turtle (fish) net: 2 item netting^x + vertical end sticks + float sticks^x
              + float fiber tassels^x + float tassel-float stick fiber binder^x + stone
              sinkers^x + stone sinker-mesh binders^x

wounded previously by the other variety of pig arrow, which had a
greater number of components. This form had a wooden shaft, and its
separate wooden foreshaft was fitted into the shaft and held taut by a

piece of cord covered with beeswax (Fig. 4–1c). Both ends of the wooden arrow shaft were bound with fiber thread to prevent them from splitting. These binding units are considered as separate and distinct since the one at the proximal end of the shaft was designed to prevent the nock from splitting, whereas the lashing at the opposite end was to prevent the fore-shaft socket from splitting. Into the split distal end of the foreshaft a trianguloid point ground from a shell was inserted; at the base of the point were two lateral bone barbs. Fiber thread was wound around both the point and the barbs to bind them to the foreshaft, and a length of fiber line was tied below the barbs and to the upper part of the shaft. The effective range of a pig arrow was about fifteen yards. When the form with a detachable point struck a pig, the point cut into the flesh, and both the point and the barbs held in the flesh. As the pig fled, the foreshaft worked free of the shaft socket, but the shaft remained attached to it by the linking cord. The shaft caught in the undergrowth, and the pig was thus restrained until the hunter arrived to kill it with the first variety of pig arrow.

One of the problems in attempting to fathom the origins of forms or their components is to establish particular precursors. In terms of one general thesis developed in this study, it is presumed that natural forms most often were the archetypes or analogues. It is pertinent to note that the stingray bones used as points for fish arrows were serrated naturally. The advantages of using such a weapon point obviously were realized by the Andamanese. It does not seem farfetched that these bones might have served as models for making multiple artificial barbs on weapon points, and yet this particular innovation did not occur among these people.

The pig arrow with a detachable point is a very logical improvement on the fixed-point form. Apparently the latter remained in usage, however, because wounded pigs could be most easily killed with it. It will be recalled that only those varieties with the greatest numbers of components are considered in the comparative subsistant totals. Therefore, in the case of Andamanese arrows only the one with a detachable point is counted.

Although the six-component bow of the Naron is close in component number to the seven-part Andamanese bow, the Naron arrow had only five components, whereas the most complex Andamanese form had eleven components. Why the difference? In the dense jungle of the Andaman Islands an arrow designed with a detachable point held by a cord to the shaft functioned well because of the shaft's holding effect, but the form probably would not have been very effective in the open deserts of southern Africa. On the other hand, the poison used by the Naron on their arrows was adapted to use in their habitat. Thus, we conclude that these were forms developed as each peoples adjusted to their settings, which is hardly remarkable since this is true of the basic technology for all ongoing cultural systems. This issue is raised partially to caution against using only a few specific types to indicate the complexity of groups from widely separated areas. Instead, it seems much wiser to confine long-distance comparisons to the order level, at which differences are far more significant.

Facilities, tended. Here for the first time we encounter nets, which in this instance are designed for use in water. Netting is judged as a two-component form and as a simple facility in every instance of its occurrence. These people made dip nets which women and girls employed in taking fish and prawns in streams and along the coast at low tide. The handle and netting hoop were formed from a continuous piece of creeper which was bent back onto itself and lashed to form a handle. It is assumed that a fiber cord was used to lash the netting to the hoop. In order to more readily take fish and prawns with a dip net in streams, the poisonous seeds of a plant were crushed and thrown into the water.

Another form of net was set across the mouth of a stream to entangle turtles and fish as they were driven by men beating on the water. It seems that a second usage was to set such nets offshore. When the floats were agitated, indicating that a creature was caught, the net was hauled into a canoe. In both instances, this net was a tended facility. A set net (Fig. 4–1b) was made from fiber mesh which was wrapped around and tied to vertical sticks at each end in order to spread the mesh. Along the upper edge of the net were tied short sticks with fiber tassels lashed at the top. The stone sinkers at the bottom were tied with fiber rope to the lowest line of mesh. It should be noted that as is the case with all other facilities, whenever components are duplicated, as are the vertical end sticks, float parts, and sinkers, each is considered as only one unit.

The final form of "facility" is a leister which consisted of twelve splints of wood bound together near the handle end and separated at the opposite end to form impaling points (Fig. 4–1a). This particular leister had seventeen different parts, of which twelve were the duplicative impaling point-handle components. It appears that a large number of points were required in order to most effectively take small fish in confined areas; in a sense, the tidal pools were themselves facilities. The component total, if each prong is considered separately, is far greater than that encountered in any other leister known, and it grossly distorts the item's complexity. Thus, the form is classed as a facility, in violation of the letter of the classification but acceptable in the spirit of the analysis as it has been conceived. It might be added that this is the only instance in which a form knowingly has been placed in an "incorrect" subclass because its component number, distorted by duplicative parts, does not reflect its degree of complexity.

AIDS

One natural aid was a bee repellent which was made by crushing and chewing the stems of a particular plant. The mixture was smeared over the body of a person preparing to take honey from a nest of bees. The raider also held some of the mixture in his mouth and sprayed it on any attacking bees. When seeking green sea turtles or fish at night, the people were aided by fire. Their torches were made from resin wrapped in a large leaf. The only artifactual aid was the outrigger canoe, which appears to have been employed in setting and tending nets as well as in searching for fish and other marine species to shoot with arrows.

It is pertinent to note, at least as an aside, that the refuse middens at Andamanese camps contained thousands of quartz pebbles from which probably tens of thousands of blades had been struck. If one knew nothing about the grooming habits of these people, it might be assumed that stone blades were extremely important cutting tools. This was true only in a very limited sense. Stone blades were employed to sharpen boar tusks, cut fingernails, and scarify the bodies of persons. Their most important function, however, was to cut hair. Each week or ten days women shaved their heads with these blades. The women, who were the primary users of the blades, also did the flaking.

Associations. The Andamanese subsistant total of nine forms was used in the following combinations of forms from different orders or with aids.

night netting at sea: torch/ set net/ club/ canoe
night fishing: torch/ bow & fish arrow/ canoe
day netting at sea: set net/ canoe
stream netting: set net/ bow & fish arrow
honey collecting: bee repellent/ adz

From the dietary estimate of Man we know that the digging stick, fruit-picking hook, adz, and bow and arrow, each employed for a specific purpose, enabled the Andamanese to obtain the bulk of their food. It would appear that while the number of associations among them was comparatively large in terms of those identified among peoples discussed previously, they were not of paramount importance in Andamanese subsistence activities.

INGURA

Near the western shore of the Gulf of Carpentaria in northern Australia is Groote Eylandt. On this island and other nearby smaller islands lived the Ingura. When they were studied by Norman B. Tindale in 1921–1922, these people still followed their ways of old, although they had had fleeting contact with Europeans for many years and considerable prior contact with persons on Malayan vessels, who visited the area in order to obtain trepang, pearls, sandalwood, and other local products (Tindale 1925–1928). Although most Malay-Ingura contacts were hostile in nature, the Ingura did welcome trade axes, knives, and nails. The Ingura were divided into two groups of one and two hundred persons each, and together they occupied a land area of about 1000 square miles. Their settlement pattern was unusual. Initiated but unmarried males lived in one set of camps with a few old men, and most of the other people lived in separate camps. Young men gathered their own food, but the old men among them received food from women camped elsewhere. This camp arrangement almost certainly developed in response to efforts by the Malay to seize the Ingura women.

The sea and tidal swamps furnished most food resources, and therefore the people usually camped along bays, streams, and swamps. The most important species taken from the sea were dugong and hawksbill turtles. Agile wallabies were plentiful in the island interior but were not often hunted because of the stamina required for their successful pursuit. Other foods included the eggs of birds, reef fish, and a wide variety of fruits and nuts. From Tindale's descriptions it is quite clear that food resources were bountiful on the littoral of the islands.

The Ingura data occasionally will be expanded by citing objects reported among the Wikmunkan, who lived on the eastern shore of the Gulf of Carpentaria and were essentially without European contacts when studied. Their manufactures have been described by Ursula H. McConnel (1953–1955), who conducted field studies in 1927, 1928, and 1934. The Wikmunkan lived in an area that was rich or richer in food resources than that occupied by the Ingura.

NATUREFACTS

Instruments and weapons. Naturefacts employed as instruments were reported among the Seri, and they also occur among the Ingura. When an Ingura located a bee's hive in an inaccessible rock crevice, he searched for a long, thin stick which he then twisted into the honeycomb. Removing the stick he sucked the honey free and repeated the process. The use of a naturefact as a weapon is reported for the first time among the Ingura. Tindale noted that stones were thrown at small birds. The use of hand-hurled stone missiles as natural weapons probably occurred far more frequently than is noted in ethnographic reports, although kills made in this manner might not contribute significantly to the food supply of any particular people.

ARTIFACTS

Instruments. The Ingura dug up wild "yams" and other roots with digging sticks sharpened to a point at one end. Some holes from which yams were retrieved were up to a foot in diameter and four feet in depth. The Wikmunkan made two forms of digging sticks, which seem to have served partially distinct functions. A short variety was used for digging up roots, and a longer form served to obtain roots, strip bark from trees, or dig up burrowing creatures such as goanna and bandicoots. The Ingura used a flaked stone knife which they received in trade from the mainland as a general woodworking tool and also apparently to cut away tree bark in order to reach the hives of bees.

Weapons. All Ingura weapons were complex; they did not make or use the boomerang, missile stick, club, or simple shaft spear. All spears were propelled with the aid of a throwing-board of which there were three varieties, one with four components and the others with five parts each. Each was made of wood and appears to have had a wooden spear-holding peg attached to the body with fiber and gum binders. A rectangular form with five components (Fig. 4–3a) appears to have been used more com-

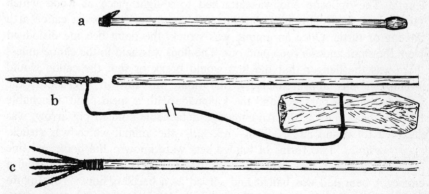

Figure 4–3.   Ingura subsistants: *a* throwing-board, *b* harpoon dart with a float, *c* leister.

monly than the other one with an equal number of parts. Wallabies some-times were hunted with a spear consisting of a wooden shaft pointed at one end, but they were not pursued frequently because they were difficult to approach and other food sources were more readily available. It is worth noting that when men practiced hurling wallaby spears, the targets were set up ten to fifteen yards away from the point at which a spear was launched.

Leisters in at least three varieties were made, but two forms with five parts each differed from one another only in terms of the weight of the wood used in the shafts. The shaft was of heavy wood when used in shallow water or buoyant wood for deep water usage, and it usually had two unilaterally barbed wood points. The third leister variety, considered as the unit type, had as many as five points which were made from the caudal spines of stingrays (Fig. 4–3c).

As the Ingura made light and heavy-shafted leisters, the Wikmunkan fashioned hunting spears with either light or heavy wooden shafts. The heavy-shafted forms were used against large game such as kangaroo, wal-laby, and emu, while those with light shafts were used against fish and birds. In addition short-shafted spears are described as serving as weapons against men or against wallaby hunted from a distance. It is even more notable that some spears had as many as four separate wooden points with a barb attached to each and were used for hunting wallaby, emu, jabiru (a tropical stork), and fish. The diversity of species taken with such a spear is much broader than would be anticipated.

The Ingura harpoon was used against fish, turtles, or sea mammals and consisted of a very long wooden shaft with a barbed point fitted into a hole (socket) at the distal end of the shaft (Fig. 4–3b). Near the base of the point was tied one end of a rope which was some thirty yards in length. The opposite end was attached to a light piece of wood which served as a float. This harpoon dart was hand hurled from a canoe at a dugong or turtle. Once an animal was struck, the point became dislodged from the shaft and the rope paid out. The float was held in the canoe unless there was the danger that the line would break or that the canoe would swamp; if this appeared likely, the float was thrown overboard, the wounded quarry pursued, and the kill made with a spear. The detachable harpoon head, just as the Andamanese detachable-pointed pig arrow, was designed to wound and restrain—not kill—the animal which was struck.

Facilities. Two forms of tended sets were known: the hook and line for fish and a weir. The fishhook assembly was used for taking fish from a canoe. A bent nail was baited and served as a barbless hook. The Ingura knew of no other hook form since they had long obtained nails for this purpose from the Malay or from wreckage which drifted ashore. At high tide the Ingura constructed fish weirs at the mouths of tidal streams by

Table 4–2 Ingura subsistants and their components.

Naturefact
  implement
    instrument
      simple
        1 component
            honey-removing stick
    weapon
      simple
        1 component
            missile stone for birds
Artifact
  implement
    instrument
      simple
        1 component
            digging stick
            stone knife (T) (bee's nest remover)
    weapon
      complex
        5 component
    ┌ ─ ─ ─ rectangular throwing-board: wood body + wood peg + fiber body-
    │   peg binder + gum body-peg binder + cane reinforcing strip
    │   ───
    │   7 component
    └ ─ ─ ─ bone-pointed leister: wood shaft + 5 naturally barbed stringray bones
                + shaft-bone binder

        5 component
            dugong harpoon dart: wood shaft + barbed wood point + point tang
                string + point-float rope + wood float
  facility
    tended set
      simple
        3 component
            fish weir: tree branches^x + grass^x + leaves^x
        4 component
            fish hook: bent nail (T) hook + bait + fiber line + line-hook binder
    untended set
      simple
        2 component
            fish-catching platform: paperbark platform + supporting sticks^x

---

combining tree branches, grass, and leaves. A narrow opening was left at
one side, and as the tide ebbed, fish were forced to swim through the passage and were taken with leisters.

A simple untended facility was employed in order to take grey mullet, which ascended a particular stream in great numbers at the end of

February. During their journey these fish were forced to swim up a water-fall some four feet in height. At the base of the falls a sheet of paperbark was supported on sticks, and the large numbers of mullet which fell backward out of the falls landed on the platform. Note that this form did not require the presence of man to function, but at the same time, it is technologically simple in design.

AIDS

One means for hunting wallabies involved the use of fire. A semicircular area of dry grass was set on fire, and hunters were stationed along the unfired side to spear animals as they attempted to escape. Dingoes were used by the Ingura to catch and kill small animals as well as to serve as scavengers around camps.

In his Ingura ethnography Tindale recorded a number of instances in which human hands alone appear to have been used to obtain food. In order to procure nectar from bottlebrush plants, the flowers were struck, and the nectar which sprayed into the palm of one's hand was licked. Sea turtle and crocodile eggs and mollusks were apparently dug up by hand; tortoises also seem to have been taken by hand. The underground nests of mound-building scrub fowl were dug by hand. At a depth of as much as six feet, the eggs of the young birds were retrieved. When a small fish was hooked a man killed it by crushing the head with his teeth; a larger fish was killed with a blow from a throwing-board.

Associations. The list of Ingura associations is numerically comparable to that reported for the Andamanese.

    leister fishing: canoe/ leister & throwing-board
    sea hunting: canoe/ harpoon dart/ throwing-board
    weir & leister fishing: weir/ leister & throwing-board
    hook & line fishing: canoe/ hook & line
    land hunting: fire spear & throwing-board

Unlike the Andamanese, the Ingura appear to have depended heavily on canoes in their food-getting efforts. Although the number of associations is the same for both groups, those of the Ingura were far more important in their overall subsistence efforts than were the Andamanese ones.

PITAPITA

The Pitapita of northwestern Queensland in Australia were described by Walter E. Roth (1897), who observed them during the years from 1894 to 1897 when he was stationed in the area as a surgeon. Although his enthnography includes information about six peoples, Roth was careful to distinguish which tribe he was discussing at any particular moment, and the Pitapita information has been isolated insofar as possible. These people lived along streams and rivers in the Boulia district and built relatively permanent oblong dwellings framed with poles. Brush was woven between the poles to form sloping sides, and over this was placed grass, then mud, and finally a second layer of brush. These were much more permanent habitations than those reported for any of the peoples discussed heretofore. Judging too from the diverse food products which were reported locally, it appears that the Pitapita were relatively sedentary in their round of seasonal activities.

NATUREFACTS

Instruments. The only natural form used directly for the procurement of food appears to have been a stick with which honey was obtained if it could not be reached by hand.

ARTIFACTS

Instruments. Only three instruments were produced. One was a digging stick with a wedge-shaped point at one end. It was used mainly by women, not only to excavate roots and tubers, but also to obtain frogs, iguanas, and snakes from their burrows. The second form, a pole with a natural hook at the end, was used for breaking off the branches of a particular species of eucalyptus tree in order to obtain the seeds. The third instrument was an ax with a ground-stone blade which was obtained in trade. The blade was hafted to a bent-stick handle and held in place with resin. The hafting technique was similar to that of the Arunta ax except that the handle was bound together in two places. The primary subsistant use of the ax was to remove honey from nests in hollow trees.

Weapons. The returning boomerang was used only as a toy. During a game one person threw it and the other participants attempted to avoid being struck on its return flight. This variety was of the same general form as the ordinary boomerang (Fig. 4–4b) which the Pitapita used for hunting as well as fighting. Another form was most often employed in fights with other people. The second simple weapon was a missile stick (Fig. 4–4d) which was thrown short distances. It cannot be established clearly from Roth's descriptions whether particular forms of spears were used solely for hunting, for fighting, or served both purposes. The most reasonable interpretation is that the shaft spear with a sharp point at one end

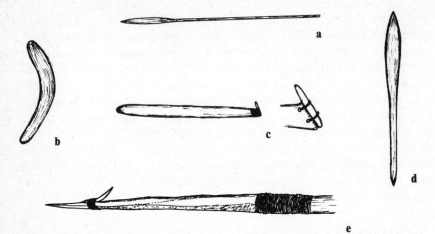

Figure 4–4. Pitapita subsistants: *a* shaft spear, *b* boomerang, *c* throwing-board, *d* missile stick, *e* spearpoint.

Table 4–3   Pitapita subsistants and their components.

Naturefact
  implement
    instrument
      simple
        1 component
            honey-removing stick
Artifact
  implement
    instrument
      simple
        1 component
            digging stick
            hooked, seed-collecting pole
        5 component
            ax (woodworking, honey removal): ground stone blade (T) + bent
                wood handle + resin blade-handle binder + 2 string handle binders
    weapon
      simple
        1 component
            pointed (lanceolate) shaft spear
            boomerang
            missile stick
      complex
        4 component
      ┌ – – – throwing-board: wood shaft + wood end peg + sinew shaft-peg
      │   binder + resin shaft-peg binder
      │ ───
      │ 8 component
      └ – – – barbed spear: wood point + wood barb + sinew barb-point binder +

wood foreshaft + sinew point-foreshaft binder + wood shaft + sinew foreshaft-shaft binder + resin foreshaft-shaft binder

facility
  tended set
    simple
      4 component
        fish net: 2 netting^x + net end poles^x + netting-pole binder^x (A)
      6 component
        portable blind & bird snare: blind boughs^x + brush^x + body attachment rope (A) + pole + quill snare + bait
      7 component
        bird guide & net: guide brush^x + saplings^x + twigs^x & 2 netting^x + end poles (A) + net-pole binder^x (A)
      9 component
        emu lure & guide & net: hollowed log lure & brush^x + boughs^x + sapling^x guides & 2 netting^x + end posts^x + net-post binder^x + forked poles^x as mesh spreader
    complex
      6 component
        bird net & water hole: artificial water hole^x + 2 netting^x + pegs^x at base of net + pole + pole-net binder (A)
  untended set
    simple
      4 component
        fish weir & trap: stone^x weir + stone^x platform + boughs^x + grass^x trap
    complex
      4 component
        pitfall: pit^x + boughs^x + saplings^x + sand

---

was for hunting as also was true of the form with a lanceolate point (Fig. 4–4a), both of which were hand thrown.

The throwing-board (Fig. 4–4c) consisted of a wooden shaft some two and a half feet in length. At the distal end a wooden peg was attached to the body by lashing sinew through two holes drilled or burned in the shaft, and this lashing was covered with resin. The spear (Fig. 4–4e) propelled with a throwing-board had a spatulate wooden point with a lashed-on wooden barb. The point was loosely bound to the foreshaft so that the foreshaft would not split on impact; the foreshaft in turn was attached to the shaft of light wood.

Facilities, tended. Compared to the peoples described previously, the Pitapita used many more varied and elaborate facilities. One simple tended set with two separate but linked parts was employed to take various kinds of birds. In order to take bustards a man concealed himself by tying boughs and brush to his body. He carried a long pole with a quill fashioned into a slip knot and tied to it; at the end of the pole or possibly in the noose a grasshopper was attached as bait. When the hunter was near enough to a bird for it to reach for the grasshopper, the hunter slipped the noose over its head and strangled it. One variation of this technique used to take birds such as cranes and ducks was for a hunter to tie leafy bushes around his head and wait in the water until a bird swam near enough for him to slip the noose about its neck. Similarly, nesting birds were approached quietly and strangled with a snare fastened to the end of a pole.

Nets were used to take species from the air, on land, or in the water. A number of different types of nets were made for emu, a bird which appears to have been important in the Pitapita diet. One technique was for men to wait near a trail used by these birds, or by kangaroo, on their trips to a particular water hole. After an emu passed by, the hunters erected nets across the trail and stationed men at points along the trail where the birds might bolt and flee. When the emu returned along the trail, they were driven into the nets and killed with boomerangs or missile sticks. Another emu-netting technique involved the use of a net in conjunction with converging lines of interwoven bushes, boughs, and saplings. The birds were lured into the open end of a funnel by the call of a concealed hunter: the sound was made by blowing into the end of a log hollowed out with fire to form an open core about three inches in diameter. After the emus had started into the trap, hunters suddenly appeared from behind and drove them between the guides to the net, where they were killed with boomerangs or missile sticks. This lure-guide-net combines the most components and therefore is listed as a unit type.

Small gregarious birds were netted near water holes after converging guides, made of brush, saplings, and twigs, were erected some forty feet in length and up to ten feet in height. The birds nested in trees at the open end of the guides, and early in the morning they were awakened by missile sticks and boomerangs thrown overhead by the hunters. The birds appear to have thought they were being attacked from above by hawks, and they flew low between the converging guide fences. At the end of the guides two men held a fine-meshed net which entangled scores of birds.

Birds that flew in flocks were taken on the wing with boomerangs. Another means for capturing pigeons, which flew in flocks, was to make an artificial water hole near a real one and use it in conjunction with a net. The lower edge of the net was attached to the ground with forked twigs, and the upper edge was attached to a long pole, one end of which was near the hands of a hunter concealed in the bushes. In the late afternoon when the birds came to drink they went to the artificial water hole, apparently because they thought that the water in it was fresher than in the natural water hole. After many birds had begun drinking at the artificial hole, the men flipped the net over and captured them.

Fish were taken in hand-held nets. Four nets were often used in conjunction with one another; each was manipulated by two men as others guided the fish into them.

Untended sets. Two different means for taking species in the absence of man prevailed among the Pitapita; one was for taking fish and the other for capturing emu. As the floodwaters of a river began to recede, a stone weir was constructed across the stream, and stone platforms were built at intervals on the downstream side. The platforms were covered with brush and then with a layer of grass. As fish descended the river through breaks in the weir, they became entangled in the grass and brush. Alternatively a net might replace or supplement the platforms.

Not only were emu netted, but they were also tracked and speared, hunted with the aid of dingoes, or, if they happened to appear in large numbers, surrounded by men and women and driven to a water hole where they were killed with missile sticks, boomerangs, or spears. Another technique for taking emu was to dig a pitfall near plants on which they were known to feed. The dirt from the excavation was carried some distance away to avert any suspicion, and the pit was covered with boughs, saplings, and sand. This untended set was constructed during the middle of one day and checked the following morning. Undoubtedly, any trapped emu were speared to death or killed with missile sticks.

AIDS

Among the anatomical aids was the practice of walking carefully along muddy sections of a river until a species of "catfish" was felt with one's feet. It was then held with the feet until it could be picked up and killed, no doubt by biting the fish just behind the head. Ants were obtained by standing or stamping on their nests. As the ants crawled up the legs of the collector, they were brushed into the hand and eaten. Freshwater mussels were located by feeling for them with one's feet and then apparently picking them up by hand. Hand retrieval appears to have been the norm for taking crayfish and for collecting berries, fruits, and many other plant products. In order to take a pelican a man might sit in a water hole or stream and conceal himself with brush or an overhanging tree limb. He then threw a series of mussel shells in the direction of a swimming bird, who drew increasingly nearer because he apparently thought that the splashes were made by jumping fish. The man then tapped the water surface with his finger in imitation of a jumping fish, and as the pelican swam still closer, it was hit with a boomerang or even killed by hand.

Among the natural aids was the use of a stone, or one's fingers, to tap a tree trunk to determine whether or not a section was hollow and might contain a bee's nest from which honey could be removed. If the nest was

suspected of being higher in a tree, toeholds were cut into the bark with
an ax, which was also used to cut the wood away to reach the hive. Emu
were hunted with the aid of dingoes, and during rainy weather when kangaroo could be forced to run over boggy ground, they too were run down
by dingoes. Finally, fires were set to encircle flocks of bustards, which
were killed with weapons after they had been asphyxiated or thoroughly
confused.

Associations. In comparison with the associations identified thus
far for other peoples, those of the Pitapita were quite well developed.

bird net & guide: brush guide/ boomerang (missile stick)/ hand-held net
honey retrieval: stone tree tap/ ax to aid in climbing and removing honey/
   stick for reaching honey
kangaroo net: net/ missile stick (boomerang, spear)
pelican lure: mussel shells (fingertips on water)/ boomerang (hand kill)
bustard hunt: fire/ missile stick (boomerang, spear)
emu pitfall: pit/ spear (missile stick)
emu net: net/ boomerang (missile stick)

These associations must be judged as more complex in their configuration
than any cluster encountered previously, because they are more numerous
and involved the integrated use of both weapons and facilities.

This is a fitting point at which to consider facility complexity in
greater detail. Note that five of the seven facilities were tended sets,
meaning that man's presence was required in order for the forms to function. The two untended sets, the fish weir-trap combination and the emu
pitfall, were the only subsistants which worked for a Pitapita in his
absence. Note too that the only complex set was the net used to cover
pigeons at an artificial water hole. This is a questionably "complex"
usage since the net did not change form when employed; only its positioning was altered.

COMPARISONS

These peoples lived in tropical settings which differed considerably
from each other. The Andamanese area was a tropical rainforest, the
Ingura lived in a tropical savanna, and the Pitapita region is possibly
best classed as tropical steppe. Both the Andamanese and Ingura were
islanders, while the Pitapita occupied a riverine setting. Each locality
appears to have had comparatively little seasonal variation in terms of
food resources. This judgment is based on the virtual absence of long-
term food preservation techniques and storage devices. The species taken

Table 4–4   Andamanese, Ingura, and Pitapita subsistants compared.

	ANDAMANESE	INGURA	PITAPITA
Naturefact			
implement			
instrument			
simple		honey-removing stick	honey-removing stick
weapon			
simple		missile stone	
Artifact			
implement			
instrument			
simple	digging stick hook-ended crabbing stick fruit-picking hook adz	digging stick stone knife	digging stick hook-ended pole ax
weapon			
simple	club		shaft spear boomerang missile stick

complex	bow & arrow	leister & throwing-
		   board
		harpoon dart
			spear & throwing-
			   board

facility			
tended set			
simple	leister dip net & poison turtle net	fish hook assembly fish weir	fish net portable blind & bird snare bird guide & net emu lure & guide & net bird net & water hole
complex			
untended set			
simple		fish-catching	fish weir & trap
complex		platform	emu pitfall
Type Totals	9	9	15
Component Totals	45	30	63
Associations	5	5	7

appear to have been largely nonmigratory, but they might occur in small herds or flocks. In each area the ordinary pattern was for men to hunt and women to collect on a day-to-day basis.

Minimal subsistant inventory for tropical foragers. On the basis of data summarized in Table 4–4, the following list of essentials is derived:

  3 simple instruments: digging stick, removing stick or pole, cutting blade
    (adz, ax, knife)
  1 complex weapon: bow & arrow or spear & throwing-board
  3 facilities

These seven essentials, supplemented by production tools and by a carrying container, would comprise the basic material culture survival kit for
foragers in the tropics. The occurrence of both instruments and weapons
suggests that pure hunting or pure collecting economies were not viable
in the tropics during early historic times. These data suggest further that,
unlike the peoples in desert areas, those in the tropics may have survived
without any simple weapon, although they may have required a greater
number of facilities (1 in the deserts *vs.* 3 in the tropics).

  Subsistant complexity. The combined total of subsistant types for the
Andamanese, Ingura, and Pitapita is thirty-three. Over one-third, or thir-
teen, of these types were comprised of a single component (compared with
a total of 29 forms and 13 one-component types of desert area peoples).
This again suggests the highly functional utility of some one-component
types, although the percentage is slightly lower in tropical areas. The
component total for the Andamanese bow and arrow in its most complex
form was eighteen, while the Ingura and the Pitapita spear and throwing-
board had at their greatest complexity totals of twelve components. Thus
the bow and arrow apparently lends itself to greater elaboration than does
the throwing-board and spear combination.

  Associations. The Andamanese and Ingura totals of five each and
the Pitapita total of eight support the suggestion that more diverse usages
were likely to develop when particular species were exploited intensively.

  Overall complexity. The usages of the Pitapita unquestionably were
the most advanced of the three tropical area peoples compared. The
Pitapita had nearly twice as many forms as either of the other two, and
their objects were used in more associations. The Andamanese rank next
because their number of components per type was far greater than that
found among the Ingura.

  Additional comments. Among the peoples of tropical regions, as
among those in deserts, we find that the subsistants of certain Australians
were more complex in their manufacture and usage than were those of
some non-Australians. Thus the often-heard generalization that aboriginal
Australian technology is "simple" when compared with other foragers
around the world is not valid for the present sample.

FIVE

Temperate Region Peoples

The desert or jungle habitats of the peoples just discussed were similar in one major respect: in both settings, food resources were relatively constant throughout the year and were obtained largely on a day-to-day basis. Sometimes, however, striking seasonal differences in harvests were noted, and there were times during a year when sustenance was less plentiful than at others. For hunters in temperate regions the seasonal differences were more extreme and seemingly led to abrupt changes in the availability of food in general, producing periods of hunger. We might expect that since seasonal contrasts are more marked in temperate habitats than in deserts and jungles, a wider range of subsistants would be required in these areas. With these presumptions in mind, we turn to foragers in temperate environments. The hunters chosen for discussion represent very different temperate settings. They include the aborigines on the island of Tasmania located to the south of Australia, the Yahgan at the southern tip of South America, and the Owens Valley Paiute of eastern California. The Tasmanians and Yahgan occupied humid temperate zones, while the Paiute lived at the margins of the Great Basin in a region probably best considered as an undifferentiated highland setting. The Paiute are judged to be in a temperate habitat because of the extensive grasslands and marshlands in their locale, the well-watered streams that existed there, and the seasonal contrasts which prevailed.

TASMANIANS

Of all the aboriginal peoples discovered and described, none are more remarkable in their cultural ways than the Tasmanians. In many respects their unique position is based on what they did not do or have. They did not make pottery nor manufacture metal products, which is not particularly unusual in terms of activities among foragers, but of greater significance, they did not employ the spear and throwing-board combination, the boomerang, or keep dingoes, even though each of these characteristics was found in adjacent Australia. They did not make bows and arrows, could not kindle fire, and did not consume any of the fish which were abundant in coastal waters and present in the rivers. *In technological terms they did not have any complex weapons, nor did they make any composite instruments or weapons.* These factors set the Tasmanians apart from all other peoples in the world.

When the British first settled Tasmania in 1803, the aboriginal population was nearly 4000, and the *last* aboriginal Tasmanian died in 1876! The beastly treatment which they received from many white settlers and sealers who visited the coasts is almost beyond belief. Yet in the dismal history of British-Tasmanian relations are interspersed certain major humanitarian efforts made on behalf of these people. The most notable of these was carried out by George A. Robinson (1966), a builder by trade, who was commissioned by the government to induce the aborigines to leave their homeland and settle on Flinders Island, where they could best be protected from hostile whites. Robinson ranged widely over Tasmania between the years 1829 and 1834 contacting some bands who had never met whites before. The journals which he kept are filled with valuable ethnographic information. Although it would be desirable to describe the subsistants of a single band, this is impossible because of the limited record. Thus, a composite is offered with the most important known regional differences noted.

These people went about naked except in cold weather; then they wore skin cloaks and sometimes moccasins. They moved often from one camp to another, and their only dwellings, built next to campfires, were windbreaks shaped with brush and sided with bark. Their most important foods appear to have been kangaroo, wallaby, and opossums killed by men and shellfish collected by women. Judging from Robinson's descriptions their only production tools were knives made from flaked stone.

NATUREFACTS

Instruments and weapons. A stick which does not appear to have been modified in any way was used to dig into a platypus burrow, and the same type of instrument presumably was used for digging up edible roots. Stones are reported as having been thrown at ducks, swans, and snakes in order to kill them. Stones were also used to batter and beat down the trunks of grass trees, which then were stripped of edible leaves.

Figure 5–1. George A. Robinson's drawing of Tasmanians climbing trees (Courtesy of the British Museum).

ARTIFACTS

Instruments. The most important instrument, at least among some coastal dwellers, was a stick sharpened at one end and hardened by fire; this was used by women for dislodging large shellfish from rocks. A woman dove for "mutton fish" and dislodged them from the rocks to which they were attached with her stick. Each one was placed in a basket made from rushes which was suspended over the woman's shoulders as she dove. Women were capable of staying under the water for a comparatively long period of time, and they did not return to shore until their baskets were filled.

Weapons. Only two simple weapons were fashioned, a spear and a missile stick. Manufacturing a spear was quite simple. The hunter selected a long pole, cut the point with a flaked stone knife, peeled away the bark, held the shaft over a fire to heat it, straightened the shaft by biting it with his teeth, and hardened the point in a fire. The missile stick, some eighteen inches in length and made from hardwood, served as the major

Table 5–1   Tasmanian subsistants and their components.

Naturefact
  implement
    instrument
      simple
        1 component
            tree-chopping stone (tree notcher) '
            digging stick
    weapon
      simple
        1 component
            hand-hurled stone
Artifact
  implement
    instrument
      simple
        1 component
            shellfish dislodging stick
    weapon
      simple
        1 component
            shaft spear
            missile stick
  facility
    tended set
      simple
        2 component
            tripping device: $grass^x$ + $grass^x$
            hunting blind: tree $branches^x$ + dead $wood^x$
        5 component
            bird lure: $pole^x$ (A) frame + $grass^x$ cover + bait + stone
            + bait-stone attachment (A)
    untended set
      simple
        2 component
            crossed spear set: $spears^x$ + ground mounting $holes^x$

---

weapon in fights. Robinson noted that these sticks were thrown with such accuracy that they seldom failed to strike their mark. One particular usage in acquiring food was to hurl a missile stick at an opossum in the branches of a tree in order to knock it to the ground.

Facilities. Among the most interesting of Tasmanian subsistants is the small cluster of rather unique sets. On an open plain frequented by kangaroo, tussocks of grass were tied together in order to trip these animals as they were chased by hunters. This "facility" is in a sense an aid and would be so classed except that the grass was purposefully tied and directly restricted the movement of game. Although the description is not complete, it appears that they made a hunting blind from branches of trees and dead wood. Here they employed spears as weapons when kangaroo passed nearby. Peoples who occupied the southwestern portion of the island made and tended a particular set for birds. It appears to have consisted of a pole framework large enough to accommodate a man and was covered with grass. At one side, or at the top, was an opening, next to which bait was placed. The bait seems to have been a fish which was tied to a stone to attract a crow or worms spread out for a duck. When a bird landed to eat the food, it was grabbed by the man inside the shelter and killed. Another set consisted of a spear mounted in the trail of a wallaby or kangaroo. The spearhead faced upward and probably was set at an angle. Sometimes two such spears were crossed and were mounted adjacent to one another in the ground. The purpose was to impale an animal and hold it in place or kill it. This is a rather clear example in which the taxonomy fails to accommodate the function of a form. The spear was a weapon but was not handled by a man in its use, and although it might hold a kangaroo in the manner of a facility, it was more likely to kill or seriously wound the animal.

AIDS

Opossums lived in tall eucalyptus trees which were climbed with two aids. One was a stone used to bruise the bark for toeholds, and the second was a grass rope which was tied around the tree trunk and the lower part of a man's legs in a single loop. By leaning back against the rope a man was able to climb from one toehold to the next. In a number of instances people obtained food only with their hands. For example, toadstools were picked and eaten, and fungus growing on trees was broken off and eaten. Men swam after platypuses and caught them by hand; eggs were collected from nests, and in some instances kangaroo appear to have been run down. Finally, fires were set to drive game from wooded areas, and a hollow log containing opossums was set on fire to smoke them out.

Associations. Once again it must be stressed that the subsistants recorded for the Tasmanians represent a composite for all the island's population. It is a certainty that the list of ten items cited was not used in its entirety by all segments of the population. The actual inventory for any particular band probably was smaller. The same may apply to the number of associations identified.

kangaroo (wallaby) hunting: grass tripping device/spear (missile stick)
hunting blind: fire/spear (missile stick)
opossum collecting: grass rope tree-climbing aid; stone for notching bark
shellfish collecting: basket/dislodging stick

The Tasmanians possessed the simplest of subsistants among the early historic foragers described herein because they did not make any complex forms and none of their weapons consisted of more than a single part. The associations likewise reflect a low level of subsistant integration. The fact that they never used more than two objects in any subsistant combination supports the assertion that they had reached a comparatively low level of technological accomplishment.

YAHGAN

These are the first people discussed whose subsistence pattern focused almost entirely at the sea's edge. They depended on their canoes not only in moving from one camp site to another but in many critical food-getting activities. In further contrast with foragers described previously, the Yahgan subsisted almost entirely on a meat diet. Their aboriginal population is estimated at 2500, and they lived mainly along the southern coast of Tierra del Fuego Island, which was the southernmost human habitat in the world. The main island was covered with dense undergrowth beneath thick stands of trees, which made overland travel extremely difficult. Snow might fall at any season of the year, winter temperatures often dropped below freezing, and summers were cool with abundant rainfall. Initial contact with the Yahgan was made in the seventeenth century, but because their location was remote, they retained many of their traditional customs into the present century. Their population declined steadily, however. The Yahgan were studied most intensively by Martin Gusinde (1961), who lived among them as a missionary and ethnographer between 1919 and 1923. He was an excellent observer and recorded details of what he saw. The range of information about their subsistants seems more complete than for any of the other peoples discussed. The major failing of this account, as of many others, is that regional differences usually are ignored. Thus the information provided is a composite for the people as a whole, rather than the more desirable detailed discussion of a single band.

A typical dwelling for a small family in the western sector was dome-shaped with a framework of bent poles covered with the most convenient material at hand, usually bark, grass, skins, or a combination of these materials. In the east where the country was more open and the winds often severe, the Yahgan built cone-shaped structures by leaning the trunks of trees together and caulking the openings between the poles. Earth sometimes was removed from the interior of either of these dwelling forms and was replaced with a layer of branches, bark, or grass. In the

Figure 5–2. Fuegian launching a harpoon (from Hyades and Deniker 1891).

center of a house a hearth was built, and around it family life was focused. Either type of Yahgan house seems ill-adapted to the setting. The fire in the fireplace actually offered the greatest protection against the cold. In milder weather men habitually went naked and women wore only a small pubic apron, but when it was cold, persons of both sexes wore short, rectangular skin capes. A cape covered only the back and was tied with a thong beneath the chin; capes also served as covers when sleeping. Additional protection from the elements was gained by coating their skin with a thick layer of grease which had been mixed with a red pigment prepared from burnt clay.

A man, his wife, and their children traveled alone or with a few other families from one camping spot to another, but they remained at a locality only a few days if food resources were scarce. There were no permanent settlements, and many persons camped at one spot for an extended period of time only when a whale was killed or discovered on a beach. Families were free to set off on their own at any time, and thus most subsistence activities were on an individual or familial basis. The animals and birds on which they depended most for food were available throughout the year in relatively stable numbers, and as a result people rarely stored food. Periods of hunger did occur, however, if a family had exhausted the food resources at one camp site and was unable to venture elsewhere by canoe because of adverse weather conditions; yet the Yahgan as a whole are not known to have suffered famines.

NATUREFACTS

Instruments and weapons. Considering the exactness of Gusinde's descriptions, when he writes that a "short stick" was used to dig up surf clams, he probably refers to a stick used without modification, and the same is likely true of those sticks used to kill fish trapped at low tide behind weirs. Occasionally, seals, apparently elephant or South American

Table 5–2   Yahgan subsistants and their components.

Naturefact
  implement
    instrument
      simple
        1 component
            clam-digging (fish-killing) stick
            sap scoop, mussel shell
    weapon
      simple
        1 component
            hand-hurled stone for birds
            seal-killing rock
Artifact
  implement
    instrument
      simple
        1 component
            mussel-removing stick
      complex
        6 component
            crab tongs: shaft + split stick tongs + leather shaft-tongs binder + 2 split wedges + wedge-tong split binder
    weapon
      simple
        1 component
            club: wood section (A)
        3 component
            dagger: wood handle + flaked stone point + handle-point binder
            seal (whale, large fish) spear: shaft + barbed bone point + shaft-point binder
        4 component
            bird (fish) spear: shaft + 2 barbed bone points + shaft-point binder

```
complex
   2 component
┌──── bow: wood shaft + sinew string
│     ──────────────────────────────────
│
│  6 component
└──── arrow: wood shaft + ground slate (chipped stone, bone) point +
          sinew (leather) shaft-point binder + 2 feather vanes + gut shaft-
          vane binder
```

   4 component
       harpoon dart: shaft + short (long) bone dart head + thong binder,
          distal end of shaft + thong head-shaft binder (or hand-held line)
   10 component
       bird sling (fighting weapon): leather pocket + 2 sinew strings + 2
          pocket-string stitchings + 2 string end leather attachments + 2
          string end leather attachment stitchings + hurling stone
facility
   tended set
      simple
      3 component
          goose snare line: sinew thong + posts^x supporting thong + baleen
             snares^x tied to thong
          fish weir: vertical poles^x + horizontal rods^x + brush^x pole-rod filler
      4 component
          fish line assembly: line + tied-on stone weight + quill with slip knot
             + bait on slip knot
      5 component
          bird snare pole & blind: pole + baleen snare loop + sinew pole-
             snare + sticks^x + brush^x blind
          herring trap: bent stick rim + vertical stick^x framing + horizontal
             mesh^x + mesh-rim-stick binder + dipping pole
   untended set
      simple
      6 component
          cormorant gorge: post + sinew lines^x + gorges^x + bait on gorges^x
             + seaweed covering^x + fat^x as sea gull lure

fur seals, were found sleeping on a beach, and if a club were not handy, a medium-sized stone might be picked up to strike and stun the animal. Sometimes too these people killed birds with stones hurled by hand. In the spring of the year they might scrape away the bark of a young tree with a mussel shell and collect the sap by pressing the shell upward; this was one of the very few techniques known for obtaining anything sweet.

ARTIFACTS

Instruments. According to Gusinde, shellfish were to the Yahgan as bread is to a European, and two species of mussels were especially important in their diet. The beds with the largest mussels were along the coast below the low tide mark. When coastal waters were turbulent and it was impossible to reach these beds, women were forced to obtain smaller mussels which could be found immediately adjacent to the shore. These were torn free by hand or broken loose with a stick which was fashioned to a wedge at one end. The technique for obtaining the larger mussels was to paddle a canoe to a bed at low tide and retrieve shellfish with the aid of tongs. The tongs consisted of a long handle of heavy wood tied with a leather thong to a short piece of flexible wood which had been hewn to a chisel shape and split partway along its length. In order for the tongs to remain open, a wooden wedge was lashed at the upper end of the split. During the time of collecting mussels, a man kept the canoe in place above the bed, or else the vessel was tied to a floating mass of seaweed. The woman probed the bottom until she had wedged a mussel shell between the prongs, and then she lifted it upward. A form rather similar but with four prongs, a unit type (Fig. 5–3e), was used by a woman in a canoe to squeeze and hold crabs or sea urchins as she lifted them upward. The crabbing tongs also were used to push a particular species of mollusk, one with a short spiral shell, from deep to shallow water where it could be picked up by hand.

Weapons. It is mentioned that a club was used to kill snared birds and also seals cornered on the beach; the form is not described but is presumed to have been fashioned from a single piece of wood. If a herd of seals were discovered on a beach, men might cooperatively separate a small cluster from the rest and club them to death; otherwise, clubs appear to have been used by lone hunters. Most peoples did not use daggers as weapons against game, but the Yahgan employed such a form. A chipped stone point was lashed to a short handle (Fig. 5–3a), and it was used mainly to kill sea lions found on the beach. The typical spear for taking large immobile creatures had a long shaft with one barb on the bone head. It was thrust by hand and served mainly to kill seals on shore. Less often, these spears were used to severely wound an exhausted whale or to take large fish in shallow coves. In addition to this form there were two other types of spears: one was used against birds and the other for taking comparatively small fish. Since the latter two were similar in form, they will be considered as varieties of a single type. Each had either one or two bone points which were barbed and lashed onto a wooden shaft (Fig. 5–3c). The birds most often sought were four species of penguins, and these were usually taken from canoes. Sometimes a flock was encircled by a number of canoes, and men not only threw their bird spears but launched stones from slings.

The bow and arrow was important in aboriginal times but declined in significance soon after historic contact. The self bow of beech wood

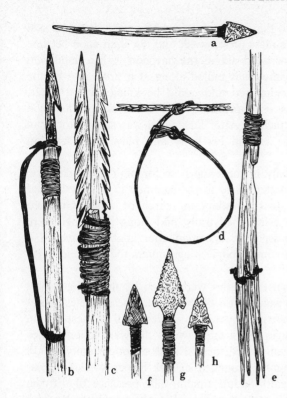

Figure 5–3. Yahgan subsistants: *a* dagger, *b* harpoon dart, *c* bird spear, *d* goose snare, *e* crab and sea urchin tongs, *f* ground slate arrowpoint, *g* bone arrowpoint, *h* chipped stone arrowpoint.

was strung with a cord of sinew. The wood-shafted arrow was vaned with two feathers attached to the shaft with a piece of gut and was tipped with a triangular point made from ground slate (Fig. 5–3f), bone (Fig. 5–3g), or chipped stone (Fig. 5–3h). The oblong tang made on each form was hafted in a wedge-shaped notch at the end of the shaft and was bound with sinew or a leather thong. The bow and arrow appear to have been most important for taking land otter and fox which were killed for their skins. A more complex weapon was the harpoon dart (Fig. 5–3b) used against seals and less often against guanaco, otter, or fish. The long shaft was tipped with a barbed bone point which had a tang fitted loosely into a depression at the head of the shaft; the point was bound in place with a strip of leather. Near the base of the point one end of a length of leather thong was tied, and the opposite end was attached to the shaft. One variation of this type had a larger head which might have two barbs, one on each side, and was used against sea elephants and whales. The shaft on this form might be shorter, and the line was attached only to the dart head. The remaining line was held coiled in one of the hunter's hands. The form of dart with an attached shaft was especially popular for use against seals in sectors where there were masses of seaweed. When a seal was wounded, it headed for a mass of seaweed, and the shaft soon became entangled. If there was no seaweed about, the harpoon with a hand-held line was launched, and the canoe was pulled along at a brisk rate by the wounded seal until it was exhausted and could be killed with a spear, club, or a paddle. Sea lions on shore also were taken with a harpoon that had a hand-held line attached. After an animal was struck, the man tied the free end of the line around his body and played the sea lion until he could make his kill.

Guanaco were found only in the eastern sector of Yahgan country, and they might be hunted cooperatively in the summer as they descended from forested upland areas to the valleys in search of water. Guanaco traveled in small herds over established trails, and along these men were stationed. As the animals passed by, one man after another launched a spear or a harpoon dart: sometimes cooperating hunters took guanaco with bows and arrows.

Two species of large baleen whales were taken by the Yahgan, but they were not hunted in the usual sense of the word. These whales sometimes were wounded and pursued by killer whales until in desperation they entered the shallow waters of an inlet, where the wary killer whales would not follow. The Yahgan waited for just such an opportunity to kill a baleen whale. They also hunted wounded or sick baleen whales at sea, but they never pursued a healthy adult animal. The presence of a dying whale was indicated by the great number of seabirds which hovered nearby; the Yahgan came from miles away and attacked the whale with harpoon darts and spears. The partially incapacitated whale might sound and escape, or it might succumb as the Yahgan had hoped. In the latter case they towed the carcass to a sheltered spot and beached it as effectively as possible. All the people in the vicinity moved their camps to the carcass and sat around chewing the fat until the great animal was consumed, usually within less than a month.

In terms of importance for hunting, the sling ranked beneath the harpoon dart and spear but ahead of the bow and arrow. Gusinde felt that the bow and arrow had declined in importance following the introduction of hunting dogs in historic times. The sling was aboriginal and consisted of a skin pocket for receiving the stone to be hurled and braided sinew strings which were tied and then sewn to two outer edges of the pocket. The outer ends of these strings were knotted and covered by a sewn piece of leather. This "complex" weapon was very important in hunting birds which flocked together, such as penguins and cormorants. Some men hurled two, or even three, stones at a time. In local conflicts slings also were used as weapons against people.

Facilities, tended. Fish were not an important dietary item, but some marine species were taken, usually by women in canoes. Dried seaweed lines were used for small fish and braided sinew ones for larger species. A stone sinker was tied near one end, and beneath it a quill was formed into a slip knot which held a piece of meat as bait. Fishing lines were used from a canoe anchored to a mass of seaweed. After a fish had swallowed the bait the line was pulled gently upward until the fish was just beneath the water surface. The woman then jerked the line and deftly grabbed the fish as it broke the water's surface. She killed it either by biting its neck or cutting it with a mussel shell.

At irregular periods during most of the year there were runs of two species of herring. Swimming either offshore or into the beach, their arrival was announced by the circling birds which fed on them and the sea mammals which pursued them. If the herring remained some distance from shore, they were dipped from the water into canoes. The women dipped them by means of a pole held in both hands, at one end of which was a specially constructed trap with an open weave. The basket-like trap was drawn through the water in the manner of a ladle and the fish deposited at the bottom of the canoe. The pole was not bound to the trap but was slipped through openings in the rim so that it could be manipulated back and forth in the water to catch scores of fish and then lifted upward to dump the catch into a canoe. When great schools entered the bays, they ran themselves up on the beach and could be scooped into baskets by hand. Another important result of the herring runs was that men were able to prey on the birds and sea mammals feeding on these fish.

A final and unusual means for taking fish was in weirs built at places where the high tide carried water into the channel of a broad stream or into a narrow inlet. It was constructed by driving sticks into the ground, weaving rods between them, and then filling the openings with brush as the tide peaked. Alternatively, the weir might be constructed to a given height except for one opening which was closed at high tide. At low tide fish were taken by hand or killed with sticks. This method was employed only when several families were together and food was scarce.

The Yahgan employed two different types of snares, both of which required the presence of a hunter to function. One was set for species of geese that were especially difficult to approach. It consisted of a heavy, braided line of sinew stretched and tied between two posts at a grassy area where geese were known to congregate. At intervals along the line baleen (whalebone) snares were attached and placed open on the ground (Fig. 5–3d). A goose stepping into a noose was snared as it moved forward. The man setting such a snare line waited nearby until the free geese became frightened at the struggles of others and flew away. The man then killed the snared birds with a club or by twisting their necks. Individual geese, ducks, and less often cormorants and penguins were taken with a baleen snare attached with sinew at the end of a long pole. This tended facility was used at dusk, and as a bird was snared, its neck was broken quickly and quietly in order not to alarm other birds nearby. A variation on the latter technique was used for taking steamer ducks. A blind of sticks and brush was built at a place where the birds were known to rest in groups. The collector waited in the blind with a pole snare and captured one bird after another as they ventured within reach. A further refinement of this technique was to capture a male duck and tie it nearby. The captive called out as the noose moved toward it, and the other ducks then ventured near enough to be snared. Sometimes when these ducks rested on the waters of a tranquil bay, the Yahgan formed a line of canoes on the open side. They slowly forced the ducks toward the land, and when the birds were narrowly confined, the hunters hurled stones from slings as well as bird spears at the flock. Any ducks that fled up the beach were run down and killed with clubs.

Untended sets. Under certain conditions cormorants might be taken at untended sets with gorges. On level ground near spots frequented by these birds, a stake was driven into the soil, and to it were tied several lines of sinew. The midsection of a small bone which had been pointed at both ends was tied to each of the lines, and on each was skewered a dead fish. The set was covered partially with dried seaweed, and pieces of fat were scattered around. Sea gulls were attracted to the fat, and their presence induced cormorants to come and look for food. They found the fish, swallowed them, and were held fast by the gorges.

AIDS

No aid was more important than the bark canoe. Since dense undergrowth made overland travel very difficult, these people moved from one camp to another by canoe and obtained much of their food directly from canoes. These vessels were covered with sections of beech bark fitted over wooden ribs and gunwales which were crossed by support bars; the bark was sewn together and then caulked. A bark canoe accommodated about six persons and usually was paddled by women. When a man went hunting by boat, his wife often paddled the vessel. As a woman collected mussels from a canoe, her husband might help her by handling the canoe, but it was more common for two women to work together, one woman fishing from the canoe as another took crabs or sea urchins with tongs.

Men hunting seals with harpoon darts from canoes might lure their prey by whistling softly, singing in a low voice, or splashing the water rhythmically with a paddle. Penguins, too, often could be drawn close to a canoe by whistling softly. Ducks were lured toward a hunter by an imitation of their call made by blowing through a duck's bill which was carried along, as was a snare pole.

One method of hunting those birds that slept in clusters on flat land involved the use of a torch. Carrying a smoldering bark torch and a club, a man crept up on the sleeping birds. He suddenly swung the torch about until it burst into flames and then clubbed as many blinded birds as possible. On rainy, stormy nights each cormorant slept with its head tucked beneath one wing. A man crept among a cluster and grabbed one bird after another. As he seized a bird with both hands, he bit its neck, killing it without a sound. When he had killed enough, he left and did not retrieve the bodies until the following morning. The dead birds were not taken away at night for fear of disturbing the live ones; if they were startled in the night, they would not return to sleep at the same spot for some time. Cormorants nested in niches on steep rocky cliffs, and their nests usually were impossible to reach from below. Typically, access to these nests was gained by quietly lowering a man on a rope at night. As he reached one nest after another, he seized and quietly killed the birds by biting their necks. He then tied the dead birds either to a strap around his waist or to the line on which he was lowered, or he dropped them to the base of the cliff if they could be retrieved from there. Yet another means for taking cormorants was for a hunter to paint his body black and, thus camouflaged, to climb trees near the water's edge where they roosted; once again the birds were killed by biting their necks.

Anatomical aids were used occasionally by women. They sometimes dove from their canoes into shallow water to hand-pick sea urchins from the beach floor, although they more often employed crabbing tongs. Females used their hands alone in collecting bird eggs, young birds in or around their nests, edible fungus from trees, and a number of different species of berries. Other examples of anatomical retrieval of plant products include licking honey from blossoms, chewing the sweet petals of one particular flower, and sucking the sweetness from the young shoots of a particular species of grass. These and other plant foods, however, played a very minor part in their diet.

Associations. The number of associations is large, but most often they are comprised of only two units.

sealing: canoe/ harpoon dart/ whistling (singing, striking water with paddle)/ spear (club, paddle)
whaling: canoe/ harpoon dart/ spear
steamer duck hunting: canoe/ sling (bird snare)/ club

penguin (sea bird) hunting: canoe/ bird (fish) spear/ sling
bird snare pole #1: blind/ live decoy/ snare pole
bird snare pole #2: duck bill call/ snare pole
bird hunting (fishing): canoe/ bird (fish) spear
goose snare line: snare set/ club
birds sleeping on land: torch/ club
mussel (crab) collecting: canoe/ mussel (crab) tongs
line fishing: canoe/ baited line
herring fishing: canoe/ basketry trap
weir fishing: weir/ stick (hand retrieval)
otter hunting: canoe/ harpoon dart
beached sea lions: harpoon dart/ club

Yahgan associations were more numerous by far than those recorded for any people discussed previously. Over half of the number involved the use of canoes, but most called for the use of only two subsistants. Thus, it would appear that even though the number of associations is great, the manner in which they were employed was relatively unelaborated.

OWENS VALLEY PAIUTE

In central California on the eastern flank of the Sierra Nevada Mountains is a great interior basin. One of the watercourses in it, the Owens River, flows into Owens Lake and also gives the local valley its name. In this region of comparatively little rainfall, hot summers, and relatively cold winters it is estimated that some 1000 Paiute lived at the time of historic contact. Intermittently between 1927 and 1931, Julian H. Steward (1933) assembled ethnographic data about these people, but at that time most of the aboriginal ways existed only in the memories of informants. In spite of this fact he was able to obtain a reasonably detailed inventory of Paiute manufactures and the contexts in which they were used.

The Paiute dressed in garments made from dehaired deerskin. Men wore breechclouts, short-sleeved shirts, and ankle-length trousers, while women wore only short skirts. Men and women seldom wore moccasins, but in the winter they bundled themselves in capes made from rabbit skins. One of the most important Paiute foods was the pine nut, and when a year's crop was good, the people wintered in timbered mountainous localities where the nuts were harvested. Here they lived in pole-framed, double lean-tos covered with pine boughs. During a year of poor nut production, they remained at valley bottom villages, living in cone-shaped semisubterranean structures built around a pole framework and covered with earth.

Here they subsisted primarily on seeds which they had collected in the summer and fall. While at their valley settlements, the Paiute gathered seeds and hunted, with their most intensive hunts conducted in the fall. The most unusual feature of their food-getting efforts was that they constructed dams and ditches in order to irrigate plots of wild plants for greater seed harvests. The seeds were not planted or cultivated, but they were watered by artificial means. In the spring when a stream was dammed in order to divert the water into an irrigation ditch, the fish stranded in the stream bed were collected. After the fall seed harvest the diversion dam was broken and the fish stranded in the irrigation network were recovered. During the summer and fall, fish also were taken with leisters, arrows, baited hooks, basketry traps, and by poisoning large pools.

ARTIFACTS

Instruments. Bulbs, roots, tubers, and plant foods stored by rodents as well as the rodents themselves were obtained with the aid of a digging stick. To keep their irrigation ditches clear of debris, these people used a long pole. The only instrument employed for collecting pine nuts was a pole which had a wooden hook tied to the end with a leather thong. An instrument with two physically separate parts, the first such type to be encountered in this study, is the seed beater assembly, composed of a beater and a container to receive the seeds. The bundled grass used as weft and warp elements of the beater framework extended downward to form the handle, and the outer edge of the beater was framed with a section of willow (Fig. 5–4a). The cone-shaped basket (Fig. 5–4b) to receive the seeds consisted of warp and weft elements and a separate piece bound to the basketry to form the rim. This same implement may have been used to beat a species of cane at the time of year when small insects brought sweet sap to the surface. The sap was dislodged by beating the cane, and the sap granules were collected in a container.

Weapons. Clubs are mentioned only as being used by men when they drove rabbits into nets. It is assumed that they were fashioned from a single piece of wood. The only other simple weapon was a leister which was made by attaching three bone prongs to a cane shaft. The most important weapon by far was the bow, which was used with five different varieties of arrows. The standard bow was backed with sinew and strung with a cord of sinew. The arrows were shafted with willow or apparently more often with cane which was bound at both ends to prevent it from splitting. For all but the fish arrow, three feather vanes were lashed together with sinew at their proximal end and were worked into the sinew band at the nock end. The variety for taking rabbits had eight components; the duck arrow,

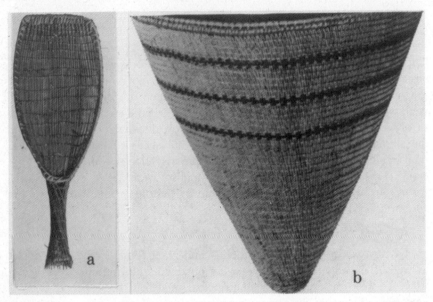

Figure 5–4. Owens Valley Paiute subsistants: *a* seed beater, *b* seed collection basket.

Table 5–3   Owens Valley Paiute subsistants and their components.

Artifact
  implement
    instrument
      simple
        1 component
          digging stick
          irrigation ditch pole
        3 component
          pine cone removing hook: pole + wood hook + rawhide pole-hook
            binder
        4 component
          seed beater: willow frame + weft elements + warp elements +
            basketry-frame binder
          seed collecting basket: wood rim piece + weft elements + warp
            elements + basketry-rim binder
  weapon
    simple
      1 component
        rabbit-killing club (A)
      5 component
        leister: cane shaft + 3 bone prongs + shaft-prong binder (A)

complex
  3 component
    bow: wood body + sinew backing + bow string

  13 component
    game bird arrow: cane shaft + 2 sinew bindings, one at each end of shaft + 3 feathers + proximal feather end sinew binder + blunted wood point + 4 crossed sticks + sticks-point binder
facility
  tended set
  simple
    1 component
      brush^x mountain sheep surround
    3 component
      deer disguise: deerskin + deer antlers + attachment to hunter (A)
    4 component
      fish hook assembly: bone hook + weight (A) + line (A) + bait
    5 component
      rabbit net: 2 netting^x + upper attachment line (A) + bottom attachment line (A) + vertical support poles (A)
      hunting blind: bent pole^x frame + pole binding^x + willow^x siding + bough^x siding + grass^x siding
    6 component
      seine: 2 netting^x + upper line attachment (A) + lower line attachment (A) + vertical end sticks^x (A) + end stick-netting binder^x (A)
    8 component
      fishing with poison & dam: poison + 4 component basketry container + stitching^x around container mouth + sod^x + stones^x for dam
  untended set
  simple
    1 component
      caterpillar trap: trench^x around tree
    5 component
      diversion dam & ditches to irrigate wild seeds: dam boulders^x + brush^x + sticks^x + mud^x & ditch^x
    7 component
      basketry fish trap & dam: 4 component basket + attachments (A) & sod^x + stones^x
  complex
    4 component
      deer (mt. sheep) trap: ?+ ? + ? + ? (AA)
      rabbit (wildcat) spring-pole snare: snare loop and line + willow trigger set + willow tether + bent birch pole
    7 component
      small game deadfall: overhead stone weight + horizontal weight support stick + vertical support stick + diagonal bait stick + horizontal stick-bait stick line attachment + bait + bait-bait stick attachment

nine parts; the fish arrow, four parts; and the form used against big game or men had ten components. The variety with the greatest number of parts was for taking game birds: it had a blunted point and four short sticks crossed and bound near the point. This thirteen-component game bird arrow is entered as the unit type.

Facilities, tended. The Paiute appear to have fashioned only one type of lure. It consisted of a deerskin and antler disguise, probably attached to a hunter's body and used by a man hunting alone. By imitating the behavior of a deer, he was able to attract an unsuspecting animal within bow and arrow range. The one form of hunting blind was a dome-shaped structure used for taking waterfowl. It consisted of bent poles bound together at the top and covered with willows, boughs, and grass.

Among the fishing methods was the practice of damming streams with sod and stones to form pools and then poisoning the water. A plant poison was prepared and encased in old baskets which were sewn closed. A number of men then swam into a pool, pulling the bundles of poison through the water. Shortly thereafter, the stupefied fish were taken by hand, shot with arrows, or impaled with leisters. Hook and line fishing involved the use of bone hooks baited with grasshoppers or worms; the hooks were probably attached to weighted lines. Nets too were used, although they are not well described. Presumably they functioned as seines, and it is likely that they had separate lines attached at the top and bottom as well as vertical sticks tied at each end to spread the mesh.

The type of net designed for taking rabbits was far more important than the fishing net. A single net was about three feet in height and up to fifty feet in length. A number of nets were set to form an arc, and in order for them to be utilized effectively the cooperation of many persons was necessary. A group of men drove the rabbits toward the nets, and as the animals became entangled or darted about in a confused manner, other individuals who were stationed there clubbed or shot them.

For taking mountain sheep or antelope the best archers concealed themselves along the trails used by these animals at the same time that other men drove them into the ambush. Another technique for capturing mountain sheep was to build surrounds of brush in narrow canyons and then drive the sheep into them so that they could be killed.

Untended sets. The most remarkable Owens Valley Paiute facility by far was the dam-ditch complex designed to irrigate plots of wild seeds. The irrigated areas were not planted, tilled, or cultivated in any manner. Areas chosen for irrigation were near a stream which could be dammed, and the water was diverted into ditches to flow over a number of plots if possible. One irrigated field measured four miles in length and was about a mile and a half wide. One man was chosen each year as the irrigator, and he was aided by about twenty-five men in the construction of the dam which was built from boulders, brush, sticks, and mud. The water was diverted into ditches which were kept clear by the irrigator. Adjacent plots were irrigated on alternative years, apparently in an effort to allow the areas to reseed themselves.

In this locality a particular form of caterpillar developed in one species of pine tree, and at a certain stage of its growth, it descended to the ground. The caterpillars' descent might be encouraged by building a smoky fire nearby. Trenches were dug around the trees, and the caterpillars fell into these as they crawled down. In the absence of men fish were taken at dam sites by attaching open-twined baskets, which became fish traps, below the dams to catch the fish as they swam downstream.

Steward's informants recalled that some form of trap, not nets or pitfalls, was used to take deer and mountain sheep, but they could not offer any details about the form. I arbitrarily have assigned this trap four components and have considered it to be a complex set. For smaller game such as rabbits and wildcats, spring-pole snares of different sizes were set. These unbaited snares were set in game trails, and when an animal's foot jarred the willow trigger, the spring pole was released, lifting the animal into the air. They also made a deadfall to take smaller game such as ground squirrels.

AIDS

One use of fire as an aid was to kindle a smudge at an animal's burrow. Apparently arrows were shot at the escaping animal or it was dug out with a digging stick. More important, however, was the use of fire in communal deer drives. Men formed a great circle, and each carried a bark torch to set the brush on fire. As the deer became increasingly confined by the fire, they were shot with arrows. Dogs were kept mainly as pets and appear to have been used only occasionally to locate and surround deer which the hunters then killed with arrows. In order to hunt ducks and sometimes to fish, men might bind tules together to form a raft. The only other conveyance probably used in hunting was a pair of snowshoes. It is reported that before setting traps men chewed salt grass and put it on their hands and feet in order to avoid leaving a human scent on the sets. Hand retrieval of food products included the collection of sunflowers and other plants such as wild onions and clover.

Associations. In comparison with the desert and tropical peoples discussed, the number of Paiute associations is great.

irrigated seed plots: dam/ ditches/ irrigation ditch pole/ seed beater &
  collecting tray/ fish by hand retrieval
fishing with poison at dam: dam/ poison bundles/ leister (fish arrow, hand
  retrieval)
deer fire drive: torches/ bow & arrow
deer drive with dogs: dogs/ bow & arrow
mountain sheep (antelope) hunting: brush surround/ bow & arrow
rabbit drive: nets/ club (bow & arrow)
burrowing animal hunting: smudge fire/ bow & arrow (digging stick)
deer lure: deer disguise/ bow & arrow
trap setting: chewed grass deodorizer/ spring-pole snare (deadfall, deer trap)
duck hunting: tule raft/ bow & arrow
waterfowl hunting: blind/ bow & arrow
caterpillar trap: trench/ smudge fire
winter hunting: snowshoes/ bow & arrow
fish dam & trap: dam/ basket trap
hook & line fishing: fish hook assembly/ tule raft

The fifteen associations identified for both the Yahgan and Paiute seem
to reflect that temperate settings are conducive to the development of many
more combinations of subsistants than are found among peoples in desert
and tropical habitats.

COMPARISONS

Desert and tropical environments are more homogeneous around the
earth than are temperate settings. For this reason, if for no other, we
would expect to find greater differences among the subsistant inventories
of peoples in temperate habitats. When the long-term cultural isolation of
the Tasmanians is considered in addition, it is not surprising that they
stand in rather striking contrast with the Yahgan and the Paiute. Because

Table 5–4   Tasmanian, Yahgan, and Paiute subsistants compared.

	TASMANIANS	YAHGAN	PAIUTE
Naturefact			
implement			
instrument			
simple	tree-chopping stone	mussel-shell sap scoop	
	digging stick	clam-digging stick	
weapon			
simple	hand-hurled stone	hand-hurled stone seal-killing rock	

Artifact			
implement			
instrument			
simple	shellfish dislodging stick	mussel-removing stick	digging stick irrigation ditch pole seed beater & collecting basket pine nut removing hook
complex		crab tongs	
weapons			
simple	shaft spear missile stick	spear club dagger bird (fish) spear	rabbit-killing club leister
complex		bow & arrow harpoon dart bird sling	bow & arrow
facility			
tended set			
simple	tripping device hunting blind bird lure	goose snare line fish weir fish line assembly bird snare pole & blind herring trap	brush mt. sheep surround fish hook assembly deer disguise rabbit net hunting blind seine fishing with poison & dam
untended set			
simple	crossed spear set	cormorant gorge	caterpillar trap diversion dam & ditches basketry fish trap
complex			& dam deer trap spring-pole snare small game deadfall
Type Totals	10	9	20
Component Totals	17	69	95
Associations	5	15	15

of the seasonal variability which prevails in temperate habitats, we might expect storage devices to be important among foragers in such settings. However, among all the peoples discussed so far, only the Paiute depended heavily on stored foods. The implication is obvious; some temperate-area peoples, like those described from the tropics and deserts, could depend on obtaining food on a day-to-day basis throughout the year.

Minimal subsistant inventory for temperate region foragers. On the basis of data in Table 5–4, the following forms were shared by all three peoples:

3 simple instruments, one of which is a digging or dislodging stick
2 simple weapons, one of which is a spear, bird spear, or leister
4 simple facilities, one of which is a hunting blind

This nine-type total may be compared with the five-type total for desert-area peoples and the six-type total for tropical peoples. A major portion of the increase, limited as it is, occurs within the facility class. This suggests that hunting blinds, lures, and traps were consistently more effective in temperate than in desert and tropical areas. It also appears that temperate-area foragers could not sustain pure hunting or pure collecting economies, a characteristic also of foragers in desert and tropical habitats.

Subsistant complexity. In combination, the Tasmanian, Yahgan, and Paiute had a total of forty-nine subsistants, and of this number seventeen, or about one-third, were formed from one component (compared to about one-half for desert peoples and one-third for those in the tropics). Thus, it would appear that the proportion of such types is consistently high among foraging peoples in any of these habitats. The greatest component totals for types by region reported thus far are the fifteen components for the Arunta spear and throwing-board and eighteen for the Andamanese bow and arrow. For the temperate peoples the highest type total recorded is the Paiute bow and arrow with a total of sixteen. Suggestively, the upper limit of component numbers for a type occurs in those with two functionally linked forms, and it probably does not exceed about twenty.

Associations. The Tasmanian total of five is inordinately small on the basis of expectations. This is explained by their very simple technology in general, or more importantly, by their isolation. By contrast the Yahgan and Paiute had fifteen associations each, which is far more than for any other peoples described thus far. The next highest is found among the Pitapita who had eight, and it will be recalled that they lived in an area which was at or very near the border between tropical and temperate areas. It appears that temperate area peoples do not have a great many more subsistants than do some desert or tropical peoples, but the forms represented are combined in many more ways. This is partial validation of the postulate that seasonal variability in a temperate setting leads to an increase in the diversity of techniques for obtaining food.

Overall complexity. The Tasmanians are considered the simplest because they had so few subsistants with a diminutive number of components, and they utilized comparatively few associations. The Yahgan and Paiute are nearly identical in type and association totals, but the Paiute are judged as more complex because their component total is far greater than that of the Yahgan (95 *vs.* 70).

SIX

Northern Peoples

In any gross classification of peoples in terms of world geography, those discussed in this chapter lived either in the arctic or subarctic of North America. They represent three very different habitats within the general area, however. The Nabesna lived in an Alaskan lake and riverine setting dominated by high mountains and coniferous forests. The Caribou Eskimos ranged over a portion of the Barren Grounds, a bleak tundra region in north-central Canada. The Angmagsalik, who also were Eskimos, lived along the eastern shores of Greenland in a locale with a polar or arctic climate. The Nabesna contrast strikingly with the Eskimos both in linguistic and cultural terms. They were Na-Dene speakers whose way of life was most often adapted to the exploitation of inland forests. The interior and coastal dwelling Eskimos were adapted to a tundra setting, and their language was of a different linguistic group. Unlike most of the hunters discussed previously, all of these peoples lived where the winters were both very long and extremely cold, and comparatively little food could be obtained during that part of the year. The highly seasonal nature of subsistence efforts was more pronounced in the arctic and subarctic than in any other major geographical region. For all three peoples hunger or starvation was an annual threat in the early spring. Although they stored food, large surpluses were so rare that they usually were unable to cache enough to last them through the long winter.

On logical grounds alone we would retrodict that hunting economies did not become adapted to the subarctic and arctic until after the essential exploitative techniques had been perfected in temperate areas. As peoples moved into northern habitats, we might expect them to employ a greater range of subsistants than have been identified heretofore. The reason is that these peoples were primarily hunters who consumed little in the way of plant products, and it is the weaponry and facilities associated with hunting, not the instruments pertinent to collecting, which have the greatest potential for elaboration.

NABESNA

The Nabesna or Upper Tanana lived beside lakes and streams feeding into the Tanana River of east-central Alaska. Their first significant contacts with Euro-Americans occurred in 1887 when a party of explorers passed through their country. Although occasional travelers and gold seekers had paused briefly in the area, the Nabesna still retained or could recall most of their aboriginal ways when they were studied in 1929–1930. The aboriginal base-line ethnography for the Nabesna written by Robert A. McKennan (1959) is the most complete study of any northern Athapaskan hunters. At the time of his fieldwork the largest band numbered fifty-nine persons, and the total population was 152. Their number probably had been somewhat greater at the time of early historic contact, but even then all of the livable area was not utilized. In the southern sector of their homeland great mountains rose as high as 16,000 feet, while the northern area was an expanse of rolling hills leading to the flat Tanana River valley. This is one of the coldest inhabited areas of North America. Winter temperatures drop to −70 degrees F. or even lower. Summer temperatures, however, may rise to 100 degrees F. These thermal extremes reflect the continental nature of the climate. Spruce forests are the dominant ground cover up to 4000 feet, while the willows and alders at slightly higher elevations are met at their upper reaches by tundra vegetation, snow, or ice. The most important large land mammals were the Barren Ground caribou and grizzly bear in the uplands, Dall sheep in the mountains, and moose and black bear in the valley bottoms. Smaller animals included arctic ground squirrel, beaver, lynx, muskrat, porcupine, snowshoe hare, and wolverine. The most important fish were the whitefishes; salmon did not ascend the upper Tanana River.

The Nabesna lived during the winter in dome-shaped, circular structures framed with bent poles and covered with sewn moose skins. With a decline in the food resources in one locality they might move camp repeatedly. During the summer they tended to remain in a single camp, at which they fished. Here they constructed rectangular houses with vertical walls of posts and with flat roofs, both portions being covered with the bark from spruce or birch trees. The people moved from one hunting area to another in small family groups during the winter, but they tended to cluster in larger numbers during the summer. The winter clothing for men and women alike consisted of a caribou skin shirt worn with trousers preferably made from sheepskin. Moccasins were sewn onto the trousers, and they wore caps as well as mittens of skin. Summer clothing was essentially the same as for the winter except that the skins were dehaired and skin boots were worn.

ARTIFACTS

Instruments. No subsistant naturefacts were identified for the Nabesna, and as we might expect, they employed very few artifactual instruments since most of their food was derived from animals capable of motion. One instrument usage is reported, and another is presumed to have been used. The Nabesna took roots from muskrat caches and dug up the roots of a particular plant in the early spring, but there is no reference to the digging implement. The not-too-distant Tanaina used a short stick for this purpose (Osgood 1937:41), and it is assumed that the Nabesna did likewise.

Thus far in the descriptions of subsistants used by different peoples, the only complex instrument identified was made by the Yahgan, but the Nabesna too had a complex form. In the winter when a bear was found in its den it was roused, and two men pinched it between two poles, which presumably were bound together at one end. While they held the bear, other men killed it with clubs or spears. As hunters the Nabesna lacked a number of forms reported among nearby peoples; for example, they did not use gill nets, hooks, gorges, or harpoons to take fish.

Weapons. The simplest weapon was a short spear made from caribou antler and used against bears. The antler was soaked in oil in order to increase its weight and thus add to its effectiveness as a club, which was its alternative use. A second variety of spear, which was also used against bears, is the unit type since it had a greater number of components. This spear consisted of a knife with a pounded copper blade set into a wooden handle which was then lashed to one end of a pole. Two varieties of leisters were used during the summer months. One form had a single barbed point of beaten copper, and the more complex unit type had a cluster of three barbed copper points (Fig. 6–1c).

The only complex weapon was the bow and arrow. The birch wood of the self bow was rubbed with a mixture of grease and squirrel blood to increase its toughness. Since these substances were necessary to the lasting qualities of the bow, and did not function simply as materials used in a manufacturing process, they are considered as a unit present in the finished form. The bow (Fig. 6–1a) was strung with a babiche (rawhide)

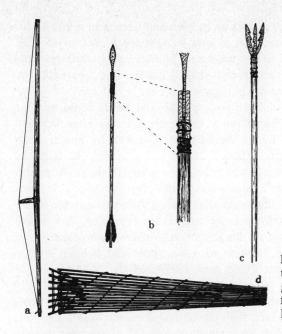

Figure 6–1. Nabesna subsistants: *a* self bow with bow guard, *b* big game arrow with foreshaft, *c* copper-pointed leister, *d* fish trap.

cord, and a piece of wood or bow guard was lashed to the inner face of the bow shaft to receive the impact of the bow string. All the arrows were spruce-shafted. Five forms of bird and small game arrows were made, with from seven to eight parts each. One big game arrow had eight components, and another variety, the unit type, consisted of nine components. All arrows had three split feather vanes, and the point, or foreshaft in one instance, was lashed to the shaft with sinew. The nine-part unit type had two pieces of bone lashed at the distal end of the shaft. Between these retaining prongs, which served as a foreshaft, was wedged an antler arrow-point with a long tang (Fig. 6–1b). On impact the point separated from the shaft and foreshaft combination.

Facilities, tended. Northern Athapaskans are well known for their different types of traps and deadfalls, and the Nabesna typify this diversity in many respects. They did not use decoys or disguises to aid them in tending their facilities. The most important source of food and raw materials was the caribou which migrated through the region in enormous herds during the early part of the summer and again in the early winter. On occasion individual caribou or moose were trailed on snowshoes and shot with arrows. The techniques for taking large numbers of caribou were far more rewarding, however. One form of caribou guide consisted of two converging lines of felled trees. At the narrow end of this funnel snares were set or hunters were stationed with bows and arrows. Caribou were taken easily once they were driven by men and women into this guide-surround. A variation was to erect a long straight fence and at intervals to leave openings in which snares were set. Moose, unlike caribou, were too wary to be driven into the funnel-shaped guides, but they could be taken in the snares set at openings in a guide fence.

Mountain sheep were difficult to approach and rarely could be shot with arrows, but they could be snared at the heads of draws after they had been driven there by men. Snowshoe hares were driven by hunters into tended tether snares. Women stationed at the sets retrieved the hares as soon as they were caught and pinched their hearts to kill them. Any hare that ran back toward the hunters was killed by the men's arrows. McKennan (1959:48) has suggested that among Athapaskans the snare has been underrated in its importance for taking big game, and in all probability he is quite correct in this judgment. Muskrats sometimes were taken by attaching a net of rawhide to a long pole and holding it at a tunnel exit or house entrance. One man frightened the animals out as another held the waiting net.

Untended sets. As is evidenced by the immediately preceding text, most snares were tended; in fact, the only untended snares were for grouse and caribou. The grouse snares were sinew nooses tied at intervals to twig fencing. These sets were made around spots where grouse dusted themselves. The caribou drag snare, a complex untended set, consisted of a rawhide line with a noose formed at one end and a log tied to the opposite end. The set was arranged so that the open noose hung over a trail at the height of a caribou's head and antlers. When an animal was caught, the noose tightened, and the drag was dislodged, to be pulled along the ground by the frightened caribou until it caught against brush or trees and held the animal fast or strangled it to death.

Facilities, not weapons, were the most important means for taking fish. Most fishing took place in July when the important species, whitefish, was fattest and migrated from lakes into streams and then into the Tanana River. The slow-moving streams were almost ideal for weir sets at which grayling, pike, and loche might also be taken. Weirs were built by driving posts into the streambed and weaving an impenetrable maze of tree branches between the posts. At the center of a weir an opening was left, and it was reached on a walkway which apparently was lashed to the weir posts. At the gap fish were taken with a dip net or in a funnel-shaped fish trap. The trap consisted of a long cone made from splints of spruce wood bound together with withes. A small inner funnel at the open end also was made of withes and probably was bound to the outer cone with the same raw material (Fig. 6–1d). Fish swam through the small opening and became trapped in the cone. The dip net had a long wooden handle at the end of a hoop to which netting made from spruce root was fitted. A dip

Figure 6–2. Nabesna man with a dip net at a fish weir (Courtesy of Robert A. McKennan).

net used at a weir was a tended set, and in this instance the dip net had five components. The cone-shaped fish trap, also with five parts, was by contrast an untended set. Given the unit type rule, either form could be entered. I have recorded the fish trap because it is a more advanced form than a dip net since a person's presence was not required for it to function.

Three types of complex untended sets were employed in addition to the caribou drag snare. Two snares which involved the movement of a pole are judged as varieties of a single type. The spring-pole variety of snare had four components and was designed to take small animals such as fox, ground squirrels, hare, and lynx. The set was made by bending a sapling, attaching to it a sinew line held in place with a toggle bar and then looping the line around a tether pole and on to form an open noose held in place with a small stick. In cold weather, because the spring pole lost its elasticity, a tossing pole set (Fig. 6–3a) was made for the same species; this form had six components and is judged as the unit type. The principle was the same as for the former variety except that a small tree trunk, probably mounted between crossed sticks, served to lift the snared animals into the air.

The samson-post deadfall (Fig. 6–3b) consisted of horizontal logs over which an animal stepped (1). The logs were held in place by two sets of vertical posts (2), between and above which a heavy log (3) was held up with a vertical stick or samson post (4). Beneath one end of the fall log was fitted a stick (5) to which bait (6) was fixed. An animal

Figure 6–3. Nabesna snare and deadfalls: *a* tossing-pole snare (adapted from Osgood 1940:239), *b* samson post deadfall, rear guide logs not included (adapted from Osgood 1940:245), *c* overhang deadfall.

Table 6–1   Nabesna subsistants and their components.

Artifact
  implement
    instrument
      simple
        1 component
            digging stick (A)
      complex
        3 component
            bear-holding poles: 2 poles + rawhide binding (A) at one end
  weapon
    simple
      4 component
          bear spear: (knife point: copper blade + wood handle) + wood
            shaft + knife-shaft binder
      5 component
          three-prong leister: 3 copper points + wood shaft + shaft-point
            binder (A)
    complex
      5 component
          bow: wood shaft + grease and blood coating + wood bow guard +
            guard-bow binder + bow string

      9 component
          big game arrow: wood shaft + 3 vane feathers + sinew shaft-feather
            binder + 2 piece bone foreshaft + sinew shaft-foreshaft binder +
            arrowpoint

facility
  tended set
    simple
      2 component
          mt. sheep (moose) snare: rawhide snare + attachment anchor
          hare snare: sinew snare + brush^{x} attachment
      3 component
          funnel-shaped caribou guide & snares: felled tree^{x} guides + rawhide
            snares^{x} + snare line-ties to trees^{x}
      4 component
          caribou (moose) guide fence & snares: fence posts^{x} (A) + brush^{x}
            (A) fencing + rawhide snares^{x} + snare line-ties to trees^{x}
      6 component
          muskrat net: 2 netting^{x} + pole handle + wood netting hoop (A) +
            pole-hoop binder (A) + netting-hoop binder (A)
  untended set
    simple
      2 component
          grouse snare: sinew snare + twig^{x} fence, with snares attached to fence
      4 component
          fish weir: weir posts^{x} + brush^{x} fencing + walkway boards^{x} + board-
            post binders^{x} (A)

      5 component
          fish trap: cone-shaped trap lath^{x} + lath binder^{x} + inner funnel withes^{x}
            + inner funnel withe binders^{x} (A) + withe funnel-cone binder (A)
  complex
      3 component
          caribou drag snare: snare line + log drag + bushes^{x} to hold snare
            noose open
      6 component
          tossing pole snare: tossing pole + pole^{x} tossing pole mount (A) +
            mount-pole binder (A) + snare line + toggle bar + pole toggle bar
            holder
      8 component
          samson post deadfall: horizontal barrier logs^{x} + 2 sets of vertical
            posts^{x} + fall log + samson post + bait stick + bait + back logs^{x}
      15 component
          overhang deadfall: parallel poles^{x} + pole binders^{x} + 1st cross pole
            bound on parallel poles^{x} + cross pole bindings^{x} + 2nd cross pole +
            trees^{x} + 2nd pole-tree lashings^{x} + free pole + cross poles-free pole
            rope + trigger + bait + pole^{x} floor + pole floor binder^{x} + guide
            posts^{x} + log^{x} overhang weights

was prevented from approaching the rear of the trap by placing vertical
logs (7) behind the entrance (omitted in the illustration). In order to
reach the bait an animal was forced to place its forelegs inside the set,
and when the bait stick moved, the samson post dislodged and the fall log

crushed the victim. If it was built to take marten and other smaller animals, the construction was relatively light, but the weight of the components was increased for sets designed to take fox or wolverine.

The second deadfall used was of the overhang variety (Fig. 6–3c) and was for taking lynx or wolverine. It consisted of a series of parallel poles lashed together (1), with a cross pole bound at one end (2). This arrangement of poles was held up by tying another pole (3) between two trees (4) and attaching a rawhide rope (5) between the two cross poles. The rope was then looped over a free pole (6) wedged on top of a trigger mechanism (7) to which the bait was attached. The set had a floor (8) of lashed poles, and other posts were laid across the back of the fall (1) to increase its weight. Furthermore, guide posts (9) were erected on both sides of the entrance.

AIDS

The only use of fire in subsistence efforts was the occasional burning over of hillsides to encourage the growth of willow shoots on which moose liked to feed. Dogs were used not only to drive moose to game fences and into the awaiting snares, but also to bring bears to bay so that they might be speared or occasionally clubbed to death. Dogs also were used to tree lynx and wolverine so that these animals could be killed, apparently with arrows. In order to take muskrats during the winter a hole was cut into the top of a house, presumably with an adz, and a hunter waited at the opening. As a muskrat appeared it was speared to death. Thus, the adz was an aid which enabled the hunter to employ a spear. One anatomical aid used was to imitate the call of a raven and thereby lure a bear, who thought that carrion was nearby on which it might feed. Presumably the bear was killed with arrows. Another anatomical aid in subsistence activities was a person's use of his hands to pick various species of berries and occasionally willow buds as well.

Associations. The list of associations identified is comparatively long because many hunting techniques of the Nabesna required the use of aids and forms from different taxonomic orders.

caribou (moose) drive: single guide fence/ dog/ snares/ bow & arrows
caribou drive: funnel-shaped guide fence/ snare sets/ bow & arrows
caribou (moose) tracking: snowshoes/ bow & arrows
lynx (wolverine) baying: treed by dogs/ bow & arrows
bear call: imitation of raven's caw/ bow & arrows
bear hold: pole tongs/ club (spear)
muskrat retrieval: adz to chop hole in muskrat house/ spear

hare drive: bow & arrows/ snares
fishing: weir/ trap (dip net)

The overwhelming stress on employing snares in association with the bow and arrow is quite apparent for Nabesna hunting and trapping techniques. One particular absence also is quite significant. Although they made small, bark-covered canoes and large open skin-covered boats as well as rafts, none of these were employed in the standard hunting and fishing activities. In fact, snowshoes were the only form of conveyance used in the direct procurement of food.

Then there are the Eskimos. Although few ethnologists would admit it, if one people could be wished out of existence, it would certainly be the Eskimos. Their presence disturbs far too many neat generalizations about hunters and collectors around the world. Most gatherers lived in very small, impermanent settlements of 50 to 100 occupants; some Eskimo villages had as many as 300 residents, and settlements often were occupied for generations. Most gatherers walked or were conveyed by boats at best; Eskimos walked, used large and small boats, snowshoes, dogs as pack animals, and dog-drawn sleds. Among many gatherers the collecting activities of women were as important as the hunting activities of men; an Eskimo woman contributed very little to her family's food supply. The preservation of food among most gatherers was difficult, but not so among the Eskimos, who froze or dried their excess. Finally, and of greatest importance in the present context, the subsistants of most gatherers were comparatively simple, whereas the Eskimos are famous for their "ingenuity" and the complexity of their technological forms.

The Eskimos must be considered in this analysis not only because they exist, but because they more than any other people "test" the taxonomy and the complexity scale. Eskimos are distributed widely, from eastern Siberia to Greenland and Labrador, and over this vast area a great deal of diversity was manifest in their cultural and social ways. It was decided to describe two groups, one comparatively simple and the other very complex. The Caribou Eskimos, who lived in a sector of the Barren Grounds in central Canada, were chosen to represent those Eskimos using the simplest of technological forms, and the Angmagsalik of east Greenland represent those with very complex technoeconomic manufactures.

CARIBOU ESKIMOS

Possibly no other hunters lived in a region where physical survival was as difficult as in the Barren Grounds of central Canada. At the time

of historic contact large sectors were without permanent human populations. The Caribou Eskimo occupants were few in number and were scattered widely across the rolling tundra country where the winters were
extremely cold and the summers cool and short. Theirs was a boulder-
strewn habitat with lichens, mosses, and dwarf willows, all diminutive, as
the most typical forms of vegetation. In human terms the most remarkable
quality of this setting was the scarcity of year-round sources of food.
Although lakes and rivers were numerous, fish were comparatively few,
and on land the only edible species present throughout the year were
ptarmigan, hares, musk oxen, and marmot. These species were seldom
abundant, and they could not be depended on as a basic diet. Survival was
possible in the Barrens only because twice a year, in the spring and fall,
vast herds of caribou migrated through the region. At other times small
caribou herds might be found but not on a dependable basis.

Unlike most Eskimos who lived along coasts and were sea-mammal
hunters, the Caribou Eskimos occupied an inland tundra setting; they
seldom ventured to the coast and rarely utilized marine resources. Their
inland way of life appears to be of a comparatively recent origin, since
the sites which they occupied do not have any appreciable antiquity.
About A.D. 1400 their ancestors lived at coastal communities where they
hunted sea mammals, especially great whales, and also killed caribou
when the opportunity arose. However, the earth's crust began to lift in
their area, and it became impossible for whales to venture into the shal-
lower waters. As a result some Eskimos moved inland to live almost exclusively on caribou, and they became the Caribou Eskimos. The pattern for
coastal Eskimos to move inland and develop a caribou-based economy
occurred repeatedly in prehistoric times; the Caribou Eskimos simply
were the last people to develop the pattern. Although they were contacted
first in their homeland during 1878 to 1880, they had changed very little
before they were studied by Kaj Birket-Smith (1929) during 1922–1923.

In the early 1920s the Caribou Eskimos numbered about 450 persons and were divided into five bands. Rarely did more than forty persons
occupy a single encampment; in fact, most settlements consisted of a few
families who were related or were close friends. Both men and women
dressed in caribou skins. The men wore two sets of garments, one with the
hair side facing inward and another set with the hair facing outward. In
the summer they occupied cone-shaped tents made of pole frameworks
over which coverings of sewn caribou skins were attached. Winter houses
were dome-shaped and were made from blocks of snow; their interiors
were warmed only with lamps so that the temperature would remain at
about 25 degrees F. and the snow would not melt.

NATUREFACTS

Weapons. A single example of a natural form serving a subsistant use was reported among the Caribou Eskimos. They sometimes hurled stones to kill ermine and ptarmigan.

ARTIFACTS

Instruments. The usual forms of instruments were not made by the Caribou Eskimos. Except for the casual collection of berries, especially by children, plant foods were not a part of their diet. They did employ two different forms of instruments against essentially incapacitated animals. Fish were killed with a bone awl to which a thong was attached; the dead fish was strung on the thong which had a toggle bar at the opposite end (Fig. 6–4b). In addition caribou which had been trapped in pitfalls were killed with antler daggers (Fig. 6–4d).

Weapons. One of the favored and most productive means for obtaining caribou was for persons to slip behind a herd and drive the animals into a body of water or for two men to move wolf skins up and down and frighten caribou into the water, where they could be speared from kayaks. The spear shafts were made from short lengths of wood which were pegged together, since long pieces of wood were not to be found on the Barrens. At the end of the shaft was a foreshaft made from antler, and in fully

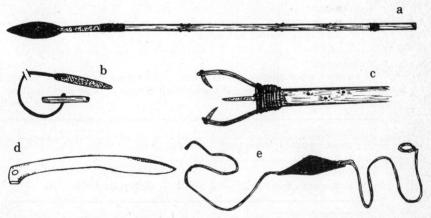

Figure 6–4.   Caribou Eskimo subsistants: *a* caribou spear, *b* fish-killing awl and toggle bar line for carrying fish, *c* two-pronged leister with central point, *d* caribou-killing dagger, *e* sling.

Table 6–2   Caribou Eskimo subsistants and their components.

Naturefact
  implement
    weapon
      simple
        1 component
            stone hurled at ermine (ptarmigan)
Artifact
  implement
    instrument
      simple
        1 component
            antler dagger
        4 component
            fish-killing awl (fish skewer): bone awl + attachment thong + thong
            loop stitching + antler toggle bar
    weapon
      simple
        12 component
            leister: 2 horn side prongs + 2 antler barbs + antler center prong
            + thong side prong-center prong-shaft binder + short wood shaft
            + shaft extension + 4 (A) wood pegs as shaft component binders
        13 component
            caribou spear: 3 piece wood shaft + 4 (A) wood pegs binding shaft
            components + 2 piece antler foreshaft + rawhide shaft-foreshaft
            binder + stone spearpoint (A) + rawhide point-foreshaft binder
            (A) + shaft-base rawhide lashing
      complex
        4 component
    ┌── bow: wood shaft + sinew backing + antler strip between shaft &
    │   backing + rawhide bow string
    │
    │ 9 component
    └───arrow: wood shaft + antler point + shaft-point binder + 4 feather
            vanes + sinew proximal feather-shaft binder + sinew distal feather-
            shaft binder

      2 component
    ┌─── throwing-board: wood shaft + end peg (A)
    │
    │ 4 component
    └─── bird spear: wood shaft + 2 points + shaft-point binder (A)

      5 component
            bird sling: 2 attachment thongs + stone pocket + sinew thong-
            pocket stitching + stone
  facility
    tended set

simple
  1 component
    stone^x cairn caribou frightener
    snow^x cairn caribou lure
  2 component
    fish lure: fish skin + attachment line (A)
  3 component
    dam & weir: stone^x dam + stone^x weir + stone weir closure
  6 component
    fish hook assembly: antler (A) hook + bone weight + bait on hook
    + bait binding to weight + line + reel
complex
  3 component
    caribou frightener: sea gull skin + stick + skin-stick binder bolas:
    antler bola balls^x + attachment lines^x + stick as toggle hold
  4 component
    caribou pitfall #1: pit^x dug in snow + brush^x cover + moss^x cover
    + urine bait
untended set
  simple
    2 component
      hare (marmot) snare: snare line + stone anchors^x
    3 component
      fox tower trap: stone^x tower + top covering (A) + bait (A)
    4 component
      gorge: sharpened bone + bait + line attachment + stone anchor
      bird snare: snare line + line attachment + support stone + tie stone
  complex
    3 component
      caribou pitfall #2: pit^x dug in snow + snow^x block walls + snow^x
      cover
    4 component
      fox deadfall: fall stone + vertical trigger stone + bait + trigger-
      bait line (A)
      wolf pitfall: pit^x + snow^x cover (A) + bait (A) + bone dagger at
      pit bottom
    6 component
      fox trap: stone^x sides + stone^x roof + stone door + trigger (A) +
      bait + bait-trigger-door line

---

aboriginal times this weapon probably was pointed with an end blade made from ground stone (Fig. 6–4a).

Arctic char were taken during the summer at fish dam and weir combinations. The leister used in association with such a facility had a central point and two lateral prongs (Fig. 6–4c). The lateral prongs were made from musk-ox horn, and the central point as well as the barbs which were attached to the ends of the prongs probably were made from antler in aboriginal times. A short wood shaft at the forward end was spliced to

Figure 6–5.   Caribou Eskimo shooting a sinew-backed bow (Courtesy of the National Museums of Canada).

a longer shaft with wood pegs. This leister was hand-hurled and was aimed so that it would strike fish at a lengthwise angle. The central prong entered the flesh from above, and the lateral prongs were pushed apart but held the fish fast with their barbs until it could be killed and removed.

The bow was the most important complex weapon used by strictly inland-dwelling bands. A typical form consisted of a wooden shaft backed by attaching sinew with half-hitches. Between the sinew and the wood was a thin strip of antler. A bow was strung with a rawhide cord. The caribou-hunting arrow consisted of a wood shaft, vaned with either two or four feathers, and headed with an unbarbed antler point. The point had a conical tang which was bound to the shaft loosely enough to work free from it and into the wound of an animal that was struck. They also used two-pronged bird spears which they hurled with the aid of throwing-boards, but neither the spear nor the throwing-board is described adequately.

Another complex weapon was the sling which served primarily as a toy but also was used by boys for taking birds. The loop in one end of the thong (Fig. 6–4e) was placed around the forefinger of the hurling hand, and a stone was placed in the sealskin pocket. As the loose end of the thong was released, the stone was hurled through the air.

Facilities, tended. While caribou hunting was the foremost subsistence activity, fishing ranked second and was especially important during the winter when supplies of cached caribou meat had dwindled and caribou were scarce or absent locally. Late in the fall an oblong hole was chopped in the thin ice which formed on streams, and a fish skin was suspended on a line facing into the current. The skin became inflated with water and was manipulated by a man as he stood poised to strike with his leister any fish that took the lure. Winter fishing was largely at lakes. Here holes were cut in the ice with antler-pointed ice picks, and the fishing was with hook and line. As fresh ice formed at a fishing hole, it was removed with a scoop made from musk-ox horn. The unbarbed hook and the weight used in such fishing probably were made from antler in fully aboriginal times. The line was attached to the weight through drilled holes and was wound on a wooden reel. For this type of fishing the hook was baited with a piece of fish skin and was tied to the weight.

Late in the fall, when caribou were fat and often abundant, they were hunted with the greatest intensity. They were likely to appear in large herds, and a number of different hunting techniques were employed against them. One was to have women and children slip behind a herd and frighten them by waving their parkas and howling like wolves. This method was used in a locality where stone cairns had been erected on adjoining ridges. The caribou were afraid to bolt up the ridges to escape because they thought that the cairns were people, and so they dashed down the valley toward the spot where hunters were concealed with bows and arrows or else plunged into a lake or stream where hunters in kayaks waited with spears. Another more favored use of cairns was to erect one long row of stone "men" and to set up between them sticks with sea-gull skins tied at the top. The caribou were so frightened by women beaters, the cairns, and the flapping sea-gull skins that they ran to escape in a nearby body of water, only to be killed by hunters waiting there with their spears and kayaks.

In the fall before the land was completely snow-covered, a cairn of snow might be built; caribou were drawn to white objects at this time. If the snow was not deep and if the caribou were numerous, a pit was dug nearby in a snowdrift. The sides were built up with blocks of snow and the top covered with snow slabs. It was necessary to tend this type of pit-fall since, given time, trapped animals would be able to escape.

The bola which these people used to take birds is classed, with some misgivings, as a complex facility. Each of the four weights in a bola cluster was made from antler, and each had a hole drilled at one end, through which a line was fastened. These lines were tied together at the opposite end, and a small stick was inserted into the knot. The purpose of the stick apparently was to prevent the lines from slipping out of the hunter's grip prematurely as he prepared to throw it. The bola was swung around and around in a small circle and then released as a flock of birds flew overhead. The bola balls cartwheeled through the air, and the lines tangled around the wing or neck of a bird, drawing it to the ground.

Untended sets. The untended pitfall was dug in deep snow, covered with brush and moss, and baited with urine. Caribou were attracted to the urine because of its salt content, and as many as three animals might become trapped at one time in a single set. Caribou taken in pitfalls were killed with antler daggers which hunters carried suspended from a line attached to their belts. An incompletely described pitfall for wolves had a bone dagger facing blade upward at the bottom of the pit. Snares, while not set for caribou, were used to take other species. For capturing hares or marmot, snares were set between stones. Another form of set was made near the nests of birds, presumably ducks and geese. A snare line was set on two stones and tied to a third stone. When a bird stepped into the noose and then moved forward, the noose drew tight about one leg.

By the time Birket-Smith visited these Eskimos they had used steel traps for so long that they had nearly forgotten the design of aboriginal traps and deadfalls. From the descriptions which they were able to give, however, the trap for fox was a box-shaped, three-sided structure built from stones. Slightly above the open end was a separate stone which had been attached to a line leading to the bait inside. When a fox took the bait, the stone door was jarred down, trapping the fox inside. They also set a stone deadfall for fox. The heavy stone used for the fall was held upright by another stone from which a line probably led to the bait. When a fox pulled at the bait, the vertical stone was dislodged, and the weight fell on the fox. It probably is legitimate also to include a tower trap made in the not-too-distant past by the members of at least one Caribou Eskimo band. The description again is inadequate, but it seems to have been a hollow tower of stones, presumably with a light covering on top on which the bait was placed. A fox jumped up to take the bait, fell through the covering, and was trapped inside the structure.

A gorge might be used in a set to take sea gulls or fish. Made by sharpening a piece of bone at both ends, the gorge had a line tied around the middle, and the opposite end was attached to a stone. A piece of fat was skewered on the gorge to serve as bait for sea gulls; a piece of fish served the same purpose for taking certain species of fish. The sea gull or fish that swallowed the bait found itself held fast by the attachment line because the gorge toggled in its stomach.

AIDS

When hunting caribou during the fall mating season, a man might hold a pair of caribou antlers over his head, and he might imitate the grunts of a bull as a lure. A male caribou who ventured near, prepared to fight a rival, would be killed with arrows. In the summer caribou were also frightened into water by men waving wolf skins. Of all the aids possibly none equaled the kayak in importance; in fact, this was its primary function in Caribou Eskimo culture since travel was rarely by water. Snowshoes were used only during a very brief period in the spring, because the snow was firmly packed most of the time. They do not appear to have been worn at all in hunting activities. The only other notable artifactual aids include the ice pick and scoop used in winter fishing and the paraphernalia associated with dog sledding as well as the sleds and dogs themselves. Dogs were few in number because of the difficulty in feeding them; two to three dogs per family appear to have been the norm. During much of the year dogs were used to pull sleds when camps were moved or when hunting trips were taken. In the summer a dog carried a pair of packs on his back, and he might at the same time drag tent poles from one camp to the next. Finally, dogs were used to bring musk oxen to bay so that hunters could move in for the kill.

Men sometimes pursued moulting geese in kayaks until the birds were so exhausted that they could be killed by hand. If a goose took to the land, it might be run down and killed by hand. These people also picked up eggs from nests and collected berries, but this food played an insignificant part in the diet.

Associations. Given the overwhelming stress placed on taking caribou and the fact that these animals were abundant for only two brief periods during a year, we would expect to find that most associations centered about this species. The second major subsistence activity, fishing, likewise has a number of associations surrounding it.

caribou drive along a row of cairns: cairns/ sea gull skin frighteners/ kayaks/ spears
summer fishing at weir: dam/ weir/ leister/ fish-killing awl (skewer)
caribou drive between rows of cairns: wolf calls/ cairns/ bow & arrows (kayak & spears)
caribou pitfall: cairn of snow/ pitfall set/ bone dagger to kill trapped animal
caribou drive into water: wolf skin disguise/ kayaks/ spears
thick ice fishing: ice pick/ ice scoop/ hook & line
thin ice fishing: ice pick/ fish skin lure/ leister
caribou lure: antlers carried over head/ bow & arrows
musk-ox hunting: dogs to bring animals to bay/ spear (bow & arrow)

The most notable dimension of these associations is the fact that more separate subsistants and aids were combined than are reported for most peoples. This suggests the highly developed or complex nature of Caribou

Eskimo caribou hunting as opposed to the food-getting specializations of other peoples. It was suggested previously that when one species provides most of the sustenance, the number of associations developed for taking it is great, and this seems especially true if the species involved is a herd animal.

ANGMAGSALIK ESKIMOS

At the time of historic contact Eskimos lived from eastern Siberia to Labrador and Greenland. Of all the separate groups, the Angmagsalik are unique in one extremely important dimension. They alone were described quite thoroughly during the first year that they were contacted, and the information about them is almost unparalleled in the annals of ethnography. Furthermore, within twenty years of historic contact a vast amount of ethnographic data had been collected about their aboriginal way of life. Occasionally prehistoric Angmagsalik Eskimos had journeyed southward along the coast by open skin boat or umiak in order to visit West Greenland Eskimo settlements and, in later years, Danish trading stations. Although the Vikings settled some sectors of western Greenland as early as the tenth century A.D., they avoided the Angmagsalik area and the eastern shore in general, as did later vessels, because of the ice masses which pushed southward along it from the arctic pack. During the early summer of 1884 a group of Danes under the leadership of Gustav Holm, a lieutenant in the Royal Danish Navy, and accompanied by Eskimos from the south set off for Angmagsalik. They arrived there late in August and settled down to a winter among these unknown people, who numbered about 400 persons. All of the ethnographic information about the Angmagsalik has been drawn from a definitive study edited by William Thalbitzer (1914).

The Angmagsalik lived on islands and among fjords which were headed by glaciers. The surrounding country was mountainous and rocky. The dominant vegetation was heaths and mosses, while in sheltered localities clumps of willows and dwarf birch grew. The area borders on a great storm center in the north Atlantic, and it is subject to violent winds and relatively heavy precipitation. In many ways life among the local Eskimos was dominated by the storis, or great jumbled masses of ice floating southward from the polar sea. The coast is largely free of ice only from August until sometime in November, when new ice begins to form, thicken, and drift back and forth with the winds. When the storis jammed against the fjords, it was impossible to hunt and people might starve; when this ice was gone, however, the sea currents often were strong and hazardous.

Yet it was the sea on which the Angmagsalik depended almost entirely for food. From it came marine animals and fish as well as the driftwood for manufactures. Flotsam was a source of metal and diverse exotic forms which arrived from the top of the world.

Marine animals were the staple source of food for these Eskimos. The bearded, harbor, and ringed seals dominated in importance. Narwhals were common at certain seasons, walrus were present but rare, and polar bears were plentiful when certain ice conditions prevailed. Diverse waterfowl frequented these waters, and there were edible fish in the ocean as well as shellfish along the coast. For variety in their diet the Angmagsalik ate berries, roots, and plant greens as well as several species of seaweed. Very few land-dwelling species were to be found, and none were important. Caribou, musk oxen, and hares were known but had become extinct locally before historic contact. As a result, ptarmigan were the most important sources of meat from the land. Caribou had been hunted with bows and arrows, but by 1884 this weapon was no longer made. The people also recalled having hunted great whales in the past, but they did not normally do so at the time of historic contact. Women did not contribute significantly to food-getting activities. They took some fish and shellfish, collected plant products, and obtained foxes and ptarmigan. It should be added, however, that women might join men in taking sharks. Under certain circumstances girls became accomplished hunters. This was most likely to occur when a man had daughters but no sons.

The Angmagsalik built large, rectangular, subterranean houses with walls of stone and turf and pitched roofs framed with driftwood and covered with sod and old skins. A sleeping and lounging platform extended the length of the rear wall. It was partially separated by dividers of skin and was apportioned to the small family units who were related or friendly with one another and occupied a house jointly. Light was provided by windows of gut and by oil-burning lamps; the latter also provided warmth and served as a source of heat for cooking. During the summer months, only very closely related families lived together in their tents which were essentially cone-shaped, framed with wood, and covered with sewn skins.

The typical clothing for a man included a sleeved and hooded hip-length sealskin upper garment or parka with the hair side facing inward. In the winter a man wore over this an additional hip-length parka with the hair facing outward. Men wore only diminutive shorts of sealskin when in the village, no matter how severe the temperature, and knee-length skin boots. When hunting or traveling they wore breeches of seal- or bearskin with the hair facing outward, and over them was drawn a pair of bearskin breeches if the man planned to hunt on the ice. A man who went out in a kayak during foul weather wore a waterproof parka of sewn gut over his inner parka. The inner and outer parkas of women were of the same general style as those of men except that a mother's parka was large in order to accommodate her infant. Women usually wore only a small pubic covering except when traveling. The short breeches they added when traveling still exposed their thighs, since their boots just reached over the knees.

ARTIFACTS

Instruments. Not only did the Angmagsalik do without naturefacts as subsistants, but they did not have any instruments of the usual types. However, they employed bone-bladed hunting knives to kill wounded animals which were incapable of escaping. The blade was long for the variety used against narwhals and short if employed against seals. The most common form had a wooden handle, often highly decorated, into which the bone blade was wedged.

Weapons. Of all the peoples discussed, the Angmagsalik had the most elaborate weapons by far and presented the greatest classificatory challenge. Considerable care has been exercised to select only the major types so that the discussion of their subsistants might parallel those for the other foragers, but it has been difficult to decide whether a form was a variety of a type or whether it stood alone as a distinct type. The leisters were judged as varieties of one type while most harpoons were considered as distinct types since components of the latter often were assembled in contrasting ways.

In the summer when large numbers of salmon ascended rivers, they were taken at stone weirs with leisters. The form of leister used (Fig. 6–8a) had a bone point extending from the shaft and two lateral bone prongs with separate bone barbs, all lashed together at the end of a shaft. It has been judged as the unit type since it had seven components, a greater number than other varieties of leisters. Another form, used against sea scorpions, had two to three multibarbed points and a component total of five. When food was scarce, it was used as an instrument for entangling and retrieving seaweed at low tide. A third variety of leister, for taking capelins from a kayak, consisted of diverging wooden splints. This form is poorly described but possibly did not have any more components than the unit type.

Each of the three sealing harpoons was configured differently and served a distinct use-specific function; thus they cannot be considered as varieties of a single type. One form, hurled with the aid of a throwing-board, was used by men hunting in kayaks. The second form was for hunt-

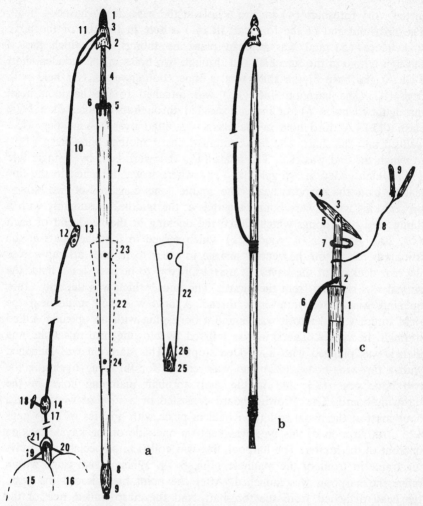

Figure 6–6. Angmagsalik subsistants: *a* toggle-headed harpoon for sealing from a kayak, *b* toggle-headed harpoon for taking seals at their breathing holes, *c* toggle-headed harpoon for "peep" hunting.

ing seals at their breathing holes in the ice, and the third type was designed for use by two men hunting through the ice.

The toggle-headed harpoon used with a throwing-board for sealing from a kayak has more components than any weapon encountered heretofore. The form is illustrated (Fig. 6–6a), and the specific components have been numbered for ready identification. The stone point (1) was attached to the toggle head of bone (2) with a peg (3), and the distal end of the ivory foreshaft (4) fit into a hole at the base of the harpoon head. The proximal end of the foreshaft fit into a hole in the top of the bone socketpiece (5) and was held in place by thongs (6) which passed through a hole in the foreshaft and through two holes in the wooden shaft (7). At the base of the shaft was a bone counterweight (8) held with pegs (9). The harpoon line (10) was attached to the harpoon head through two holes (11), and it extended through two holes in a bone clasp (12). A third hole in the clasp was fitted over a bone peg (13) wedged into the shaft. The line continued on to another bone clasp (14), to which the end was tied. The floats (15, 16) were held by a single line (17) which ended in a toggle bar (18) where it was attached to the line leading from the harpoon head. The double floats consisted of two blown-up sealskins which were bound together at the middle, presumably with a thong, and had thongs which closed the opening at the head end of each (19, 20). A section of wood (21) which served to join the floats at the front was forked on the ventral surface in order to fit over a strap across the rear decking of the kayak. If a sealskin was to be used for a float, the animal was skinned from the mouth. The anus, which was the only other opening, was closed with sinew thread. A hole was then made near the right forepaw, and into it was bound a bone plug with an opening drilled through the center. The skin was inflated by blowing into this hole, and then it was plugged with a wooden stopper. This harpoon was launched with a throwing-board (22) and was readied for throwing by fitting the two bone pegs (23, 24) in the shaft through matching holes in the throwing-board. The throwing-board consisted of a strip of wood with a bone inset at the distal end (25) held in place with a series of bone pegs (26). A harpoon of this type was kept on one side of the kayak decking in front of the hunter. The harpoon line was coiled in a special line-receiving frame in front of the manhole (Fig. 6–7). When a seal came within range the harpoon was launched. After the point had pierced the flesh, the head detached from the foreshaft, and the clasp pulled free of the harpoon line peg. As the seal sounded, the line began to uncoil from the line-receiving frame. This part of the line led back to the sealskin float on the decking behind the man, and he threw the float overboard as soon as possible in order to prevent the line from fouling. Note that this weapon combines the attributes of an implement and a facility.

When seals were hunted at their breathing holes in the ice, another type of toggle harpoon was used. The harpoon head was attached directly to the pointed distal end of the wooden shaft, and at the opposite end was lashed a bone ice pick (Fig. 6–6b). A line led from the harpoon head to the shaft where it was tied at the midsection. When a seal was struck, the head loosened from the shaft which was placed at right angles on top of the breathing hole and thus became a toggle. After a wounded seal was

Figure 6–7. Angmagsalik Eskimo hurling an open water sealing harpoon (from Thalbitzer 1914).

exhausted from the loss of blood and breath, it surfaced at the breathing hole and was killed with a hunting knife. The breathing hole was then enlarged with the ice pick at the base of the harpoon shaft so that the dead animal could be removed.

A third type of toggle-headed harpoon was used when two men cooperated in hunting seals with one harpoon. The shaft was up to forty feet in length and was made from as many as four poles fitted together with bone splicers. To one end of the pole (Fig. 6–6c) was fitted a bone socketpiece (1) which had a hole at the top to receive the base of the bone foreshaft (2). The harpoon head (3) of bone, with a separate bone blade (4), was pegged (5) into a yoke-shaped depression at the distal end of the foreshaft so that the head swivelled in the foreshaft. A line (6) was attached to the base of the foreshaft, and the bulk of its length was held coiled in a hunter's hand. A short loop of light thong was fitted around the upper foreshaft (7) and the barbed end of the harpoon head to hold the head in a nearly parallel position. A second thong (8) with two pieces of bone dangling at the loose end (9) was tied to the foreshaft. This harpoon was used in "peep" hunting, a technique employed by two men when hunting on thick ice for seals. Two adjacent holes were chopped in the ice, one large and the other small. One man lay on the ice with his head over the bigger hole and placed a skin over his head in order to see deep into the water. The harpoon shaft was placed in the smaller hole, and the peeping man guided the harpoon deep into the water with his hands. The second man stood upright and held the harpoon shaft as well as the coiled line. The pieces of bone, attached by a thong to the foreshaft, moved up and down as the harpoon shaft was jigged to attract seals. Either of the men might whistle or make other sounds as an additional

Table 6–3   Angmagsalik subsistants and their components.

Artifact
  implement
    instrument
      simple
        2 component
            hunting knife: wood handle + bone blade
    weapon
      simple
        7 component
            leister: wood shaft + 2 bone side prongs + 2 bone barbs wedged in
            side prongs + bone center prong + thong side-center-prong-shaft
            binder
      complex
        7 component
            toggle-headed harpoon, seal breathing hole: wood shaft + bone
            harpoon head + stone harpoon blade + bone head-blade attach-
            ment peg + harpoon line + bone ice pick + thong shaft-ice pick
            binder
        9 component
        ╌╌╌lance: wood shaft + bone socketpiece + bone lance shank + iron
            [drift] blade + bone shank-blade peg attachment + 2 shank-shaft
            thongs + 2 bone throwing-board pegs

        8 component
        ═══════ throwing-board for kayak harpoon or lance: wood body + distal end
            bone inset + 6 bone inset-body pegs

        9 component
        ╌╌╌╌╌ bird spear: barbed bone end point + bone socketpiece + shaft +
            socketpiece-shaft binder + 3 barbed bone side points + side point-
            shaft binder + bone base peg

        10 component
        ╌╌╌bladder dart: bone dart point + bone socketpiece + wood shaft +
            thong-socketpiece-shaft binder + bone throwing-board peg receiver
            + bone bladder holder + baleen shaft-holder binder + seagull
            crop bladder + thong crop-holder binder + wood peg stopper

        2 component
        ═══════ throwing-board: wood shaft + bone shaft receiving peg

        14 component
            salmon harpoon: wood shaft + 2 bone foreshafts + 2 bone harpoon
            blades + 2 bone blade-head attachment pegs + 2 bone toggle
            harpoon heads + 2 foreshaft-head attachment pegs + 2 foreshaft
            lead lines + retaining thong
        19 component
        ╌╌╌╌╌╌ peep sealing harpoon: 4 shaft segments + 3 bone splicers + bone
            socketpiece + bone foreshaft + bone harpoon head + bone harpoon
            blade + bone head-blade attachment pin + 2 bone head-foreshaft

```
|              yoke pins + head placement thong loop + 2 bone lures + thong
|              foreshaft-lure binder + harpoon line
|      32 component
└ ─ ─ ─ ─ -toggle-headed sealing harpoon, kayak usage: stone blade + bone
```
               harpoon head + bone blade-head attachment peg + ivory foreshaft
+ bone socketpiece + 2 thong foreshaft-socketpiece binders + wood
shaft + bone counterweight + 2 bone shaft-counterweight attachment pegs + 2 bone throwing-board receiving pegs + bone harpoon
line clasp peg + harpoon line + harpoon line distal end bone
clasp + 2 sealskin floats + thong binder of sealskins (A) + float
line + bone float line toggle + 2 sinew thread anus closers for
sealskins + 2 bone sealskin float inflation tubes + 2 thong sealskin-
tube binders + 2 wooden inflation tube stoppers + wooden float
joiner + 2 sealskin head-float joiner thongs

facility
  tended set
    simple
      1 component
        salmon weir of stones[x]
        wooden ptarmigan lure whistle
      2 component
        ptarmigan snare: snare line with loop + pole/free end of line tied
        to pole (A)
      3 component
        sea gull gorge: bone gorge + blubber on gorge + line tied to gorge
      4 component
        salmon lure: line + stone weight + bone[x] attachments + quill
        weight-lure binder
      5 component
        shark lure: line + stone weight + fat tied at end of line + seal meat
        on ice
      6 component
        mussel scoop: wood shaft + wood scoop ring + thong shaft-ring
        binder + vertical wood strips[x] + thong ring-strip binders[x] + thong
        strip-base binders[x]
      7 component
        capelin scoop: wood handle + wood mouth ring + wood base ring
        + wood vertical framing strips[x] + rawhide handle-ring binder +
        thong[x] side closure + thong[x] bottom closure
    complex
      3 component
        raven snowhouse trap: snow[x] house + thin snow[x] roof cover for bait
        support + bait
  untended set
    simple
      6 component
        sea gull snare: wood stick + snare nooses[x] wedged in stick + stone
        weight + stick-weight thong + stick top bait + bait beneath stone
    complex
      7 component
        fox deadfall: stone[x] side walls + stone[x] rear wall + large fall stone
        + strap + thong from fall stone to strap + stick + bait

attraction. When the man peeping into the water saw a seal beneath the harpoon's point, he called out "strike" to the other man, who plunged the harpoon downward into the seal. The thong loop attached to the foreshaft was forced backward as the head dislodged and toggled under the seal's flesh. The seal was played with the line, killed with a hunting knife, and removed after enlarging the bigger hole with an ice pick.

When seals resting on top of the ice were hunted, the harpoon used was nearly the same as that used in peep-hunting. The only differences appear to be in the length of the shaft—a single splice is presumed; the deletion of the bone lures, and the addition of a bone clasp on the harpoon line. The clasp was fitted on the shaft with a peg and served to hold the line taut at the head of the shaft. In addition a bone peg was fitted at the end of the shaft to catch the line held by the hunter. A man crawled over the ice, pushing the harpoon in front of him by resting the forward part of it on a small sled. The sled runners were shod with skin that still had the hair attached in order to move it as quietly as possible. When a seal was harpooned and tried to escape, the line was held by the clasp or, if it slipped out of place, by the bone peg until the animal could be killed.

In addition to the three types of toggle-headed harpoons, the Angmagsalik employed other complex weapons when hunting. Several varieties of a type of lance with a detachable point were produced. One variety which had a short shaft and was used with a throwing-board was carried on a sled during a bear hunt. A harpoon line was attached to it so that the lance could be thrown at a bear, retrieved by the line while dogs kept the animal at bay, and then thrown again. The form which had the most components was the one used with a throwing-board while hunting bear, seals, or narwhal from a kayak. This variety (Fig. 6–8c) had an iron point—obtained from flotsam—pegged to a bone shank which fitted into a bone socketpiece. Two adjacent thongs were attached from the shank to the shaft, and the point-shank unit slipped free from the shaft when an animal was struck, with the shaft serving as a drag. The only other components were two bone pegs in the shaft for receiving the throwing-board.

A man hunting from a kayak carried along a bladder dart and a bird spear as well as the standard sealing harpoon and lance. The dart was used against small seals and alternatively against birds or salmon. This weapon had a comparatively short shaft and was hurled with the aid of a throwing-board (Fig. 6–8e). The dart head of bone had a single barb (1) and appears to have been fitted tightly, but not bound, into a bone socketpiece (2) which was attached to the shaft with a thong (3) threaded through holes in the socketpiece. A bone peg (4) was wedged into the base of the shaft and fitted against the bone peg (5) mounted in the throwing-board. Near the base of the shaft a piece of bone (6) was

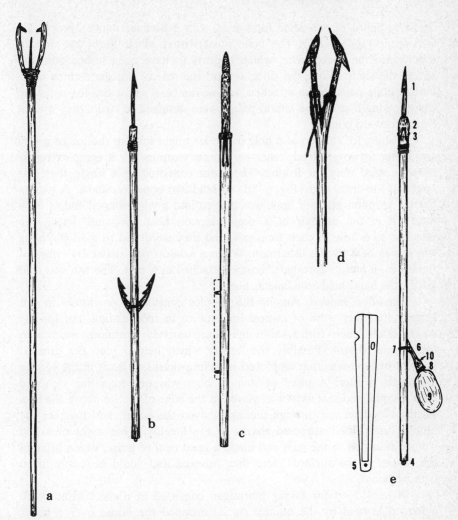

Figure 6–8.   Angmagsalik subsistants: *a* salmon leister, *b* bird spear, *c* lance with a detachable point, *d* double toggle-headed harpoon for salmon, *e* bladder dart.

bound at an angle with baleen (7). Near the projecting end of this bone was a lengthwise hole. Around a groove beyond the hole was bound (8) the crop of a sea gull (9), which was inflated and held shut with a wooden stopper (10). When the dart was thrown and struck a creature, the inflated "bladder" would float on the surface, enabling the hunter to find his prey even though the dart became partially submerged.

When swimming birds were sighted from a kayak, the hunter used a throwing-board of the same form used with a bladder dart to propel his bird spear (Fig. 6–8b). The bone point with a single barb was wedged tightly into the socketpiece, which appears to have been lashed onto the end of the shaft. Along the sides, toward the rear of the shaft, three more barbed bone points were attached, and at the base was a peg for receiving the throwing-board. The lateral points were designed to strike prey missed by the forward point.

Fishing for salmon at a hole in the ice might involve the use of a lure and either a two-pronged leister—a simple weapon—or a complex toggle harpoon used only for fishing. The latter consisted of a single shaft enlarged at the distal end (Fig. 6–8d) to hold two bone foreshafts. A toggle-headed harpoon point of bone was pegged into a yoke-shaped end of each foreshaft in the manner of a peep harpoon head. Separate lines were attached to a hole in each foreshaft, and they were tied to a single thong which was held by the fisherman. When a salmon was struck by either of the heads, it and its foreshaft became detached as a unit. The fish was held fast by the hand-held attachment thong.

Facilities, tended. Among the peoples considered previously in this chapter, facilities were of critical importance in food-getting, but for the Angmagsalik such forms, although comparatively common, were relatively unimportant. Possibly the facility which helped reap the greatest amount of food was that employed in taking sharks at leads in the sea ice during the winter. A piece of stale blubber was tied to a line weighted with a stone, and seal meat was placed at the edge of the ice above the line. As the blood seeped through the ice, it dyed the water, and together the blubber and blood attracted sharks to the locality. That night men and women returned to the spot and made a great deal of noise, which brought the sharks to the surface. Here they hovered and could be easily taken with harpoons.

A tended set for taking ptarmigan consisted of a snare attached to a long pole held by the hunter. As he dropped the noose over a bird's head, the hunter pulled the pole toward him to tighten the noose. A hunter might also lure ptarmigan by blowing a wooden whistle in order to snare birds.

A tended sea gull set was made by attaching one end of a line to the midsection of a piece of bone sharpened at both ends. A piece of blubber was placed over the bone gorge, and the opposite end of the line was held by hand. When a gull swallowed the bait, the gorge caught in its stomach, and it could be hauled in by the hunter. In order to capture ravens a small snow structure was built, and bait was placed on the roof on top of a thin layer of snow. The hunter waited inside, and when a raven landed to take the bait, it fell through the roof and was seized.

When fishing for salmon with a double-headed toggle harpoon at a hole made in the ice, the fisherman used a lure consisting of a line with a piece of stone attached to the lower end. Holes were drilled into the stone and quills inserted into them, with small pieces of bone attached at the distal ends. Salmon were attracted to these lures and then could be harpooned. Another salmon fishing technique was employed when large numbers of these fish ascended rivers in the summer. At the shallow mouths of rivers, stone weirs were constructed, and the fish were taken with leisters. When capelins were running at sea, they either were taken from umiaks with scoops or from kayaks with wood-pointed leisters. A scoop was composed of an upper and lower ring of wood, between which were vertical framing strips. Between these a thong was woven to form the sides, and more thongs were laced across the bottom ring. The scoop was held by a long wooden handle. This object is not described in detail, and it is possible that components might be missing. In order to obtain mussels women anchored an umiak along the shoreline and dipped these shellfish from the sea floor with a long-handled dipper made from wood and bound together with thongs.

Untended sets. Sea gulls were caught along the shore in small snares attached to the upper end of short sticks weighted at the bottom with stones (Fig. 6–9b). At the top of the stick was placed a small piece of blubber, and beneath the stone was set a larger section of blubber. The sea gull saw the blubber at the top of the stick first and ate it. In an effort to obtain the larger piece, it stuck its head through the noose and was strangled.

A deadfall of stones was set for fox and sometimes for ravens; it consisted of an arrangement of stones to form three walls. In the illustration of this trap (Fig. 6–9a) the lateral walls have been omitted. Above and between the walls was placed a flat stone held upright by tying a thong from it to a short leather strap fitted around the end of a stick on which

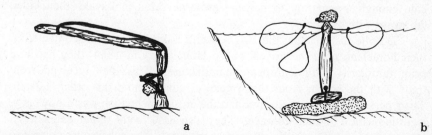

a   b

Figure 6–9.   Angmagsalik subsistants: *a* deadfall for fox with the lateral walls omitted, *b* snare set for sea gulls.

the bait had been placed. The stick was inserted into the rear wall of the set to indirectly hold the drop stone in a horizontal position. When a fox or raven took the bait, the strap slipped off the stick, causing the drop stone to fall and trap the species inside.

AIDS

The only domestic animal was the dog. It served mainly as a draft animal, with three to eight dogs harnessed to a sled. Dogs also brought polar bears to bay and were an important source of meat during periods of starvation. Imitating the sounds of seals during the process of hunting them was an important anatomical aid. In the spring when seals slept on the ice near their enlarged breathing holes the hunter imitated their sounds as he crept nearer and nearer with his harpoon in hand. At the same time he might push a block of ice before him to conceal his presence. Both techniques kept the seals lulled into a false sense of security. When attempting to harpoon seals by the peep method, particular sounds were made to attract seals to the harpooner, and when a seal was discovered on the ice, one man might attract its attention by whistling as another crept up on it for the kill. Baby seals were taken by hand, but the hunter risked receiving deep scratches.

Critical aids in seal hunting included the kayak and its accoutrements for hunting in open water, a stool to sit on when waiting for seals at breathing holes, and the small sled for balancing a harpoon when hunting on the ice in the spring. Additionally, the skin which one man placed over his head when peep harpooning served as an aid. An ice pick functioned as an aid for sealing and fishing through the ice.

Eggs and young cliff-dwelling birds were gathered from their nests by hand, and the eggs of eider ducks were picked up on flat islands. Occasionally swans could be taken by pouring oil on water where they were likely to land. After the birds had alighted, they were unable to take off because their wings slid on the oil, making it impossible for them to gain enough momentum to become airborne. Men in kayaks then killed the swans with harpoons.

Despite the fact that the Angmagsalik Eskimos were not contacted in their homeland until the arrival of the Holm party in 1884, they had had prior familiarity with European manufactures. This they received from trade with the south, from the wrecks of ships, and from other flotsam. Their possession of toothed saws and the cross-bow, which was a boy's toy, is an indication of such contacts. They also used metal rather extensively, but by and large they still were in a "bone age." The subsistants appear to reflect their aboriginal lifeway, even if some of the components, blades in particular, were sometimes made of metal.

Associations. The list of artifacts used in combination is more extensive than has been reported heretofore, and serves to stress the varying ways in which weapons were employed.

> open water seal hunting: kayak/ wood whistle lure/ toggle harpoon & throwing-board & sealskin float/ lance/ hunting knife/ eye shades
> shark hunting at edge of ice: fat bait/ meat bait/ harpoon/ hunting knife
> peep sealing in an ice field: noises made by hunters/ ice pick/ harpoon/ skin to cover one man's head
> spring hunting of seals at their breathing holes: imitation of seal sounds (block of ice, blind)/ sled/ toggle harpoon/ hunting knife
> narwhal hunting: kayak/ harpoon/ hunting knife/ eye shades
> bear hunting on ice #1: kayak/ lance/ hunting knife/ snow goggles
> bear hunting on ice #2: dog sled to reach area/ dogs to bring bear to bay/ lance (hunting knife)/ snow goggles
> seal hunting at winter breathing hole: stool/ toggle harpoon/ hunting knife
> salmon toggle harpoon: ice pick/ lure/ double toggle harpoon
> swan hunting: oil on water/ kayak/ harpoon
> capelin fishing #1: umiak/ scoop
> mussel collecting: umiak/ mussel scoop
> capelin fishing #2: kayak/ wood splint leister
> bear hunting at their dens: dogs/ lance/ (hunting knife)
> waterfowl hunting: kayak/ bird dart & throwing-board
> ptarmigan hunting: snare pole/ wood whistle lure

The number of Caribou Eskimo associations for hunting caribou pale in comparison with the Angmagsalik associations involved in seal hunting. Their open-water seal-hunting association, with its six integrated subsistants and aids, is far more complex than any association reported previously, and this is only one of several complex sealing associations. The obvious suggestion is that their usages represent a climax in the technologies of hunters.

COMPARISONS

The combined total of subsistant types for the northern peoples is sixty, while a comparable figure for those in temperate areas is forty-eight, a figure depressed because the Tasmanians had only ten forms. The totals for the Paiute (20) and Yahgan (19) clearly approximate those for northern peoples. Thus, it does not appear that there is a major break between subsistant totals for peoples in northern and temperate habitats.

Minimal subsistant inventory for northern region foragers. On the basis of comparative information presented in Table 6–4, the minimal cluster of forms for early historic hunters in northern regions is as follows:

1 simple instrument
1 simple weapon, a leister
1 complex weapon
7 simple facilities, one of which is a bird snare and another a weir
2 complex facilities, one of which is some form of deadfall

The twelve-type total is significantly greater than for any of the minimal inventories offered previously (desert area people total, 5; tropical, 7; temperate, 9). Furthermore, the number of facilities among northern hunters consistently is greater than among peoples in any other areas. Among the Nabesna and Caribou Eskimos facilities served important food-getting purposes; yet for the Angmagsalik they were far less critical except in the

Table 6–4   Nabesna, Caribou Eskimo, and Angmagsalik subsistants compared.

	NABESNA	CARIBOU ESKIMOS	ANGMAGSALIK
Naturefact			
implement			
weapon			
simple		hand-hurled stone	
Artifact			
implement			
instrument			
simple	digging stick	dagger	hunting knife
		fish-killing awl	
complex	bear-holding poles		
weapon			
simple	bear spear	caribou spear	two-prong leister
	three-prong leister	two-prong leister	
complex	bow & arrow	bow & arrow	seal breathing hole
			harpoon
		bird spear &	bird spear & throwing-
		throwing-board	board
		bird sling	bladder dart & throw-
			ing-board
			lance & throwing-
			board
			salmon harpoon
			peep sealing harpoon
			kayak harpoon &
			throwing-board

facility
tended set

simple	mt. sheep snare	stone cairn	ptarmigan lure
	hare snare	snow cairn	ptarmigan snare
	funnel caribou	fish lure	sea gull gorge
	guide & snares	dam & weir	salmon weir
	caribou guide fence	fish hook assembly	salmon lure
	& snares		shark lure
	muskrat net		mussel scoop
			capelin scoop
complex		caribou frightener	raven snowhouse trap
		bolas	
		caribou pitfall #1	

untended set

simple	grouse snare	hare snare	sea gull snare
	fish weir & trap	fox tower trap	
		bird snare	
		gorge	
complex	caribou drag snare	caribou pitfall #2	fox deadfall
	tossing-pole snare	fox deadfall	
	samson post deadfall	wolf pitfall	
	overhang deadfall	fox enclosure trap	

Type Totals	16	24	20
Component Totals	87	108	164
Associations	9	9	16

instance of the shark lure. It appears that arctic and subarctic populations could not survive without a highly varied combination of weapons and facilities.

Subsistant complexity. The three northern peoples had sixty subsistants, but only four, or less than one-twelfth of the total, consisted of a single component. This small proportion is quite striking compared to the desert peoples' inventory, of which one-half had a single component; tropics, one-third; and temperate, about one-third. One conclusion to be drawn is that in the north, unlike any other area, one-component subsistants did not play a major role in subsistant inventories. By extension, very simple forms seldom could serve man well in the north.

One of the most striking, but not surprising, observations about component numbers is that the total for all Tasmanian subsistant components is seventeen, whereas one subsistant of the Angmagsalik, the sealing harpoon used from a kayak, had forty components of its own. Even when the greatest numbers of components per form for other northern peoples are considered, this Angmagsalik harpoon is remarkably complex (Nabesna overhang deadfall, 15; Caribou Eskimo bow and arrow, 13). Yet it will be noted that fifteen of the components in the Angmagsalik sealing harpoon used from a kayak are sealskin float parts. In a very real sense, the float section is more representative of a "facility" than a weapon. Thus, this is an "ultimate weapon" among hunters.

Associations. The Nabesna and Caribou Eskimo totals of nine associations each and the Angmagsalik total of sixteen support, at least partially, a suggestion drawn earlier. This is that the number of associations increased as the subsistence activities became more specialized. Quite clearly, the varied associations for sealing among the Angmagsalik support this assertion, and the same is true for caribou hunting among the Nabesna and Caribou Eskimos. Yet why were there not more Caribou Eskimo associations connected with caribou hunting since these people depended almost exclusively on this animal for their survival? I suspect that caribou hunting techniques were more limited inherently than were sealing ones because of the diversity of conditions in which seals might be found compared with caribou. A more refined statement would be that a species which is found under differing conditions in a setting may be acquired through more varied associations than one which is always found in essentially the same physical habitat. In other words, land conditions varied little for caribou hunting, but sea conditions varied a great deal for seal hunting.

Overall complexity. The subsistant technology of the Angmagsalik was the most complex by far; their component total and number of associations both far exceed those of the other northern peoples. The differences between the Nabesna and Caribou Eskimos are not of great moment. However, I would rank the Nabesna as simpler than the Caribou Eskimos because the latter had both more components and more unit types.

Part
THREE
Evolution

SEVEN

Comparing Technologies

The primary purpose of this chapter is to rank the subsistant technologies which were described previously in detail. The ordering derived does not purport to represent the evolution of technology from simple to complex among hunters. Such a developmental pattern cannot be offered because the peoples considered herein unquestionably were far more sophisticated intellectually and technologically than any foragers at the threshold or in the early stages of culture. Nonetheless, it is implied that by comparing the specific manufactures of these peoples the logical sequence of technological achievements may be understood better than by any other means. The second aim of this chapter is to organize the subsistants discussed previously in terms of the functional purposes which they served. This makes it possible to generalize more effectively about the particular lines of diversity in technological evolution. However, before presenting the rank order for technologies and the functional clusters of forms, it is necessary to consider the taxonomy as a system and to discuss its strengths and weaknesses in terms of applications.

TAXONOMY REVIEWED

The point of departure for the entire presentation has been the idea of a "subsistant," which has proved to be conceptually and operationally satisfying. Justification for deriving this concept and originating the word was offered at the beginning of the second chapter and need not be repeated. In practical terms, such forms were isolated without difficulty. An object either served directly to obtain food or it did not, and the line between subsistants and nonsubsistants was quite clear. During trial formulations, before the concept was established with clarity, the category of carrying containers was included, but it came to be realized that such forms usually were extraneous to direct food-getting efforts. Only in rare instances did containers function as subsistants, and these usages have been identified as such (for example, the Paiute basket which received the seeds freed from grasses with a seed beater). If a container was related closely but not intrinsically to a food-getting effort, the form was judged as an association, and this secondary purpose was recognized (for example, the Tasmanian basket used for holding shellfish was associated with the collection of these edibles with a prying stick). As a means for transporting foods from one place to another, containers have no place in the subsistant taxonomy.

In retrospect I have no serious misgivings about having ignored production tools, those forms used to make subsistants and other artifacts. Another category of objects, however, has been mentioned in the introductory discussions of peoples but was not considered in the taxonomy; this is "storants," the forms used to retain food for future use. The omission is justified on the grounds that obtaining food, not carrying it about or storing it, is the most critical concern in terms of direct physical survival. Furthermore, most of the peoples discussed normally did not store foods. At the same time the ability to preserve harvests for extended periods was critical among peoples where periodic scarcities existed. Thus, I have somewhat uncomfortable feelings about having excluded storants.

The concept of "naturefact," while theoretically sound, proved to be largely unimportant in terms of the subsistants used by most peoples in the sample. The greatest significance of naturefacts is as a logical stage out of which technological developments arose, and I would hesitate to exclude this subphylum, in spite of the fact that very few subsistant forms were identified. It is only after acknowledging the naturefact-artifact distinction that the emergence of technological forms from nothing to something begins to make sense. Although naturefact subsistants were of critical importance only among the Seri, nonsubsistant uses of natural forms were quite common among the peoples sampled. These objects are identified and listed in Table 18, but only the inventories of the Andamanese, Tasmanians, and Yahgan seem reasonably complete. This list demonstrates clearly that natural objects served many purposes among foragers at the time of historic contact and that they most often were employed as tools. It does not seem presumptive to assume that these usages were far more important at earlier times than generally is recognized by paleoethnographers.

The assertion has been made that natural objects rarely had the ability to cut and that therefore naturefacts were rare as cutting weapons or instruments. The list of forms in Table 7–1 is supportive. The only natural cutting tools were shell knives, teeth, or tusks, and the naturally sharpened (fractured) stones used by the Angmagsalik to scrape seal-skins. These stones possibly were fractured by the action of coastal waves or ice. This narrow range of natural cutting tools lends considerable support to the likelihood that they probably did not occur widely at any time in man's technological history.

Possibly the reader has noted that for certain taxa in the classification there are no examples. These include naturefacts as complex instruments, complex weapons, and simple as well as complex tended and untended sets. In other words, most of the taxonomic units considered for naturefacts were not represented among the twelve peoples. It might be argued that such units should have been dropped from the classification, but I have included them because they seemed to be logical possibilities and because their absence points up potential limitations in the sample rather than "zero taxa" in the classification. For example, a hinged bivalve shell might have been used to pick up sea urchins; if so, it would have been a naturefact serving as a complex instrument. However, no instance of such usage has been located as yet in the ethnographic writings about foragers. I cannot cite an example of a naturefact which was a complex weapon, but possibly such a form existed. Naturefacts which were facilities are very much akin to natural aids; in fact, on occasion a clear line is difficult to draw between them. Conjectural instances will illustrate these points. A hunter could have hidden behind a low, natural pile of rocks and then added more stones to increase his degree of concealment. By adding stones he transformed a natural blind into one that was partially naturefactual. A fissure in the ground could trap animals, in which case the form would be a natural aid. Conceivably, a man could have torn grass free and covered the gap, thus creating a pitfall which would be a naturefact, facility, and untended set. Each of these possibilities is quite reasonable although they were not in fact encountered.

The division between the implement and facility classes did on occasion pose classificatory problems. These are best illustrated in the case of certain forms of fishing equipment. It will be recalled that implements apply human energy directly to obtain food by impinging on and physically modifying other masses. Facilities by contrast apply human energy indirectly through attracting, containing, holding, restraining, or redirecting a living mass. Fish hooks occupy a shadow zone between the two classes. Although they are usually hand-manipulated and work directly, they do not kill or seriously injure in the manner of weapons. They are not instruments, because fish are capable of motion, and yet they do not hold in the manner of a pitfall, fish trap, surround, or most other facilities.

It was decided in this and similar instances to consider such forms as facilities; if nothing else, this provides consistency.

A small cluster of implements raises disquieting questions about the proper placement of certain forms and by extension the validity of certain taxonomic distinctions which have been drawn. These are the implement types with inordinately large component numbers, many of which are duplicative. For example, the Naron game-removing hook had nine components. Duplication is represented by the four reeds bound together with three separate pieces of sinew to form a shaft of satisfactory length. The other two components were the end hook and sinew which bound it to the pole. This form is an instrument because it was hand held and used against creatures incapable of significant motion. Yet in a sense it held hares or other animals in the manner of a facility. It may well be that the implement-facility distinction should be drawn along different lines. My crite-

Table 7–1   Nonsubsistant naturefacts utilized by the twelve peoples discussed in detail.

ARUNTA
pebble stone flakers
pebbles for pecking stone
tendon removal stick
seed grinding stone
stones for kneading plant resin

NARON
drying meat on tree branches

SERI
bivalve shell digger, knife, cup, and paddle
awls of spines, thorns, and bone
deer tooth knife

ANDAMANESE
clam shell as knife, scraper, spoon
boar tusk plane
natural stone boat anchor
hammerstone
stones heated for cooking
nautilus shell canoe bail

INGURA
hammerstone, bark remover
wood smoothing pebble
stones for removing shell of fruit

PITAPITA
pounding stone
opossum tooth engraving tool

TASMANIANS
shell as cup and knife
tree bark plunged into water and water dripped from end into mouth
hammerstone
grinding stones
kelp water container

YAHGAN
flint and pyrites for fire making
grass, moss, sand, or a shell for cleaning after defecating
hammerstones for breaking bones, opening shellfish, driving wedges, pounding leather seams flat
pumice to reduce wood and bone
sandstone bone scraper
stone, coarse, for drill
stones heated for cooking
stones for crushing or kneading pigments
whetstone
shells as cups, knives, scalers, scrapers
hinged mussel shell tweezers for removing hair

PAIUTE

tree branches for storing meat
rocks on which to dry berries and seeds
cactus needle awls
hammerstones for preparing fish poison
smoothing stones for finishing wood
sand to abrade firedrill board
heated pebbles with lumps of tar to waterproof inside of baskets
stones heated for cooking
natural depression in boulder as mortar
rocks thrown in disputes

NABESNA

whetstone
heated stones for steam bathing and cooking meat
flint and pyrites for kindling fires
fungus as fire-making tinder

CARIBOU ESKIMOS

pyrites for making fires
cotton grass as tinder
naturally hollowed-out stone for a lamp
flat stone for frying meat
hammerstones to render fat into oil, break bones for marrow, and shape another stone
caribou astragalus drill bearing

ANGMAGSALIK

shell fat scraper
sharp stone fat scraper
shell as a knife
pumice skin scraper
natural cavity in a bone as a drill bearing
stones for holding down edges of skin tent
hammerstone for battering down teeth of biting dogs or for pounding pieces of iron

rion has been the direct use of human energy to physically modify a mass (implements) versus the indirect use of energy in attracting, holding, redirecting, and restraining a mass (facilities). Another approach might base the distinction between implements and facilities on the repetition of two or more components more than twice in a given form. If this procedure were followed, however, the spear of the Caribou Eskimos would become a facility because of the shaft's composite nature. Such placement would do greater violence to the "proper" classification of forms than does the unusually large number of components represented in certain implements.

The use of instruments for obtaining plant products or shellfish is quite acceptable. Certain other instances involving their employment against animals also seem reasonable (for example, the Nabesna practice of holding a semi-conscious bear with poles). Again there is a shadow zone, however: when an animal was capable of a certain amount of motion (for example, the Yahgan practice of killing a seal with a rock when the animal was on a beach from which it could not escape quickly). Occasionally, a question arose whether or not a form was a weapon or a tended set facility. The bola is an example. It did not kill or injure in the manner of a weapon, and yet it did not "hold" as do most facilities. Somewhat arbitrarily, bolas were judged as tended facilities.

At the order level the separation between simple and complex forms usually was resolved with little difficulty. This was so only after it had been decided to regard a form as complex when it had more than one component which moved. Thus, a noose snare tied to a bush was considered as simple, but a spring-pole snare was judged to be complex. In this instance I have violated the letter of the complexity definition—something that changes its physical form when in use—but hopefully I have not done violence to the quality which the concept is designed to illuminate.

In an effort to derive component totals for the subsistants used by a people, I have added the individual parts for implements to those for facilities. Yet facility components have *not* been "counted" in the same manner as those for implements. It will be recalled that if 100 stones were employed in a weir, the stones are judged as "1^x" or as representing a single component concept. It has been reasoned that to make or use the duplicative components of facilities did not require a mental template which was meaningfully different from that necessary to make or use one distinctive component. When we compare component totals for the most complex implement and the most complex facility among the peoples discussed, the summary statistics are as follows:

| | COMPONENT TOTALS FOR THE MOST COMPLEX TYPE | |
	IMPLEMENTS	FACILITIES
Arunta	15	3
Naron	11	8
Seri	13	0
Andamanese	18*	8
Ingura	12	3
Pitapita	12	6
Tasmanians	1	5
Yahgan	10	6
Paiute	16	7
Nabesna	14	15*
Caribou Eskimos	13	8
Angmagsalik	[40]	7

If we set aside the Angmagsalik implement with forty components because it clearly combines the key attributes of both an implement and a facility, then we find that the upper limit for implement parts is eighteen compared with fifteen for facilities. Since these totals are nearly the same, I feel that the decision made regarding the compatibility of implement and facility components is reasonably sound and quite operational.

The concept of "unit type" was originated in order to establish a single component number for those forms which had varieties containing different numbers of parts. An obvious example is different arrow forms; the variety of arrow with the greatest number of components was recorded

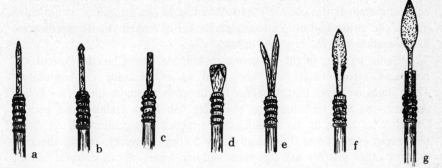

Figure 7–1. Nabesna arrowhead varieties: *a–e* small game arrows, *f* fixed
pointed big game arrow, *g* detachable pointed big game arrow
(unit type with greatest number of components).

as the unit type. In this and all comparable examples, the varieties with
lesser numbers of parts were ignored. To elaborate on one particular
instance will illustrate the reasonableness of the decisions involved.
Among the Nabesna all arrows had a wooden shaft and three split feather
vanes lashed to the shaft with sinew. Furthermore, each variety had either
one or two points attached directly, or indirectly, to the distal end of the
shaft with rawhide. Four varieties, each with a single point, were used
against small game or birds; the points probably were made from antler
in aboriginal times (Fig. 7–1a, b, c, d). Another form had two points
(Fig. 7–1e) and was used for the same general purpose as those just
mentioned. For large game the arrowpoint was made from pounded copper (Fig. 7–1f). Each of these varieties was quite similar in design and
component number. The unit type, however, was more elaborate, for it had
a foreshaft made from two pieces of bone. The arrowhead was wedged
into the foreshaft (Fig. 7–1g) and detached from it as a wounded animal attempted to escape. This form had nine components, whereas all the
others had only seven or eight parts. The principle of attachment for the
nine-component unit clearly is more complex than that recorded for the
forms with lesser component numbers. This lends support to the validity
of selecting the variety having the most parts to represent the most developed form of a type.

    Will there be further violations of the spirit or letter of the taxo-
nomic units which were not revealed among the twelve chosen people?
Unquestionably. For example, among the foraging Chenchu of south-
central India an inaccessible honeycomb sometimes was located. One
means for obtaining the honey was to tie a string to an arrow and shoot it
into the honeycomb. The honey then flowed down the string and into a
container placed underneath (Fürer-Haimendorf 1943:66). Here we have

a weapon used in a context when the employment of an instrument would be anticipated. If this example had occurred in the sample, I would have judged the string and honey-receiving basket as linked simple instruments in association with the bow and arrow.

Some persons might be prone to consider the Chenchu use of the bow and arrow which was just cited as an example of 'ingenuity." They might feel, too, that the same is true of the Pitapita means for luring pelicans, the Seri technique for obtaining fish from a staked-out pelican fed by other birds, or the Angmagsalik practice of spreading oil on water to prevent swans from flying away. My feeling, however, is that the customs of other peoples are ingenious only in terms of our cultural biases, because we never thought of certain usages. I would contend that ingenuity is a human constant, and thus need not be taken into consideration.

It would be less than candid to ignore yet another factor which possibly looms as large. If we admit that the units of the taxonomy are useful, one question of importance concerns the accuracy with which the ethnographic data have been assessed. Have subsistants been omitted? Have their component numbers always been judged correctly? Are associations evaluated with equal weight from one society to another in the sample? These are human factors in data interpretation. I have made every reasonable effort to record the various forms with precision and have analyzed the subsistants of some of the peoples numerous times. Thus, I am moderately confident about the accuracy of the recordings.

OVERALL COMPLEXITY FOR SAMPLED SOCIETIES

In Table 7–2 the subsistants of the twelve sampled societies are ranked in terms of overall technological complexity as its dimensions were defined in the taxonomy. For each people six different summary statistics as well as one ratio are provided. The six interlocking variables are: subsistant type totals; component totals; the ratio between types and components; the component number for the most complex type found in each society; the number of associations in terms of subsistants and aids; the number of tended sets; and finally the number of untended sets. Often no single factor is adequate to gauge precisely the comparative complexity of two or more technologies, because complexity in material culture evolves simultaneously along a number of different dimensions, which are reflected in the six criteria detailed. It will be presumed in the following paragraphs that the sample approximates the range for the habitats considered.

No autonomous aboriginal foragers survived into early historic times anywhere in the world on a day-to-day and year-to-year basis without a minimum of nine subsistants. I have heard stories from ethnographers of peoples with five or fewer subsistants, but have not seen documentary proof of such minimums. It is rather clear that the component total for the Tasmanians approaches the minimum of possiblities. It must be remembered, too, that the ethnographic data from which I drew my information about the Tasmanians represent diverse subgroups on the island. Thus, the seventeen-component total is no doubt higher than would be expected for some of the technologically simpler bands among them.

Apart from the Tasmanians, no people had fewer than ten parts in their most complex implement (the Yahgan bird sling had 10 compo-

Table 7–2 Ranking of subsistant technologies for the sampled societies.

	Type Total	Compo-nent Total	Types Compo-nents	Compo-nents in Most Complex Form	Associa-tions	Tended Sets	Tended Un-Sets
Angmagsalik	20	164	8.2	40	16	8	2
Caribou Eskimos	24	108	4.5	13	9	8	8
Paiute	20	95	4.7	16	15	7	6
Nabesna	16	87	5.4	15	9	5	6
Yahgan	19	69	3.6	10	15	5	1
Pitapita	15	63	4.2	12	7	5	2
Andamanese	9	45	5.0	18	5	3	0
Naron	9	40	4.4	11	2	2	2
Arunta	11	37	3.3	15	6	3	1
Ingura	9	30	3.3	12	5	2	1
Seri	9	30	3.3	13	3	0	0
Tasmanians	10	17	1.7	5	5	3	1

nents), while the smallest component number for complex facilities was three parts (the Arunta emu pitfall, Caribou Eskimo caribou pitfall, Nabesna caribou drag snare, and Angmagsalik raven snowhouse trap). The minimum number of associations is two, reported for the Naron. The Seri had no tended or untended sets, and the Andamanese had no untended sets. From these data we may conclude that no single people meets all the criteria for minimal simplicity, although the Tasmanians most nearly approach it. Thus, no one people were technologically simplest in all subsistant dimensions.

In any broad-scale ranking of the technological complexity for subsistants among the twelve chosen people, the best single measure is component totals. By considering this factor alone, it is possible to establish the general level of complexity of one inventory compared with another. *With this approach no disclaimers are necessary regarding the environment in which a people lived, the food resources which they utilized, the sexual division of labor, their physical isolation, their cultural conservatism, ingenuity, social organization, or political norms.* Overall ranks may be derived from component numbers alone more meaningfully than from any other single measurement.

In order to establish more refined rankings, other technological factors and patterns of integrated use may be considered. The Ingura rank above the Seri because they had more associations and because the Seri lacked facilities. In terms of overall complexity in material culture, there are two major clusters of foragers: those with no more than eleven forms and a forty-five component total as opposed to all others with greater totals. Thus the major break is between the Andamanese and the Pitapita, or between desert-tropical dwelling foragers and those who lived in a marginally tropical-temperate- or northern setting (the Tasmanians excepted).

Additional comparative statements add other insights. A major divider between clusters of peoples is that some emphasized the use of weapons and untended sets and lived in arctic and subarctic settings and others stressed the use of instruments and weapons, supplemented secondarily by facilities, and lived in any other earthly habitat. Peoples could not exist in nonarctic settings without the complementary use of instruments and weapons. Similarly, people could not live in arctic settings without the complementary use of weapons and facilities. By inference, instruments were relatively unimportant in the arctic, and facilities were of secondary importance in nonarctic regions.

Peoples in desert areas had four, or possibly a few more, types of facilities, most of which required the presence of men in order to function; in other words, they were tended sets. If this were true at the time of early historic contact when exploitative technologies presumably were more sophisticated than at any time previously—on a broad scale comparative basis—then it seems unlikely that foragers in prehistoric times depended as much on these forms. In other words, the farther back we push in time, the fewer facilities probably had been utilized. Similarly at historic contact people did not live in arctic and subarctic areas without having ten or more facilities. This suggests that such areas might not have been exploited intensively until such forms had evolved.

Peoples in tropical, desert, and temperate habitats did not make weapons and traps which had more than twenty components, as components have been defined. Only intensified hunters, such as the Angmagsalik Eskimos, illustrate the extent to which highly sophisticated weaponry could develop. The data further suggest that such developments were comparatively rare. In other words, very few peoples would have been able to obtain their food through the employment of weaponry alone.

If a people lived in the arctic or subarctic and employed a large number of facilities, especially snares, traps, and deadfalls, their inventory of weapons was comparatively uncomplicated. Conversely, if a people lived in the arctic or subarctic and employed a large number of weapons which were of complex design, with many components, they did not have large numbers of complex facilities such as elaborate deadfalls. Apparently if people could succeed using primarily weapons, they did not elaborate on their inventory of facilities.

The data in Table 7–2 indicate that type totals, the ratio between types and components, and the component number in the most complex forms vary to a considerable degree between the simplest and the most complex. Neither is the progression in association numbers as orderly as might be expected. Yet there is a rather steady increase in the number of sets from simple to complex assemblages. It is only the component total for each people that reflects orderly progression along the dimensions considered. This is exactly what would be expected if subsistant assemblages are integrated technological clusters in terms of their constituent parts. In the final analysis, it is not the number of subsistants, associations, or sets which are critical for establishing the comparative degree of complexity, but the number of components represented in any complete inventory of subsistants.

FUNCTIONAL PURPOSE GROUPS

Another view of technology among the foragers sampled is gained by presenting subsistants in terms of *functional purpose groups*. The aim in deriving this concept is to de-emphasize the forms in particular cultures and to stress the general means derived for obtaining food. For example, artifactual instruments include the digging stick, hook-ended crabbing stick, fruit-picking hook, and pine cone-removing hook which occur as localized types. In Table 7–3 these forms are lumped under the use-purpose label of "removing sticks." The same justification is offered for grouping the adz, ax, and stone knife, in their subsistant contexts, as "food-removing cutters."

Foragers obtained plant and animal food by removing it from the local setting. These are gathering economies as contrasted with the productive economies of farmers and pastoralists. The greatest difference between the two major economic foci is that gatherers usually did not alter the physical environment; instead, they accepted directly what nature had to offer. Exceptions do exist, as when grasslands were burned to flush animals or to promote a greater yield of edible plants, or more dramatically, when the Owens Valley Paiute diverted water to irrigate wild seed plots. Yet such practices were both rare and relatively unimportant among for-

Table 7–3   Commonly occurring subsistants categorized by functional purpose units.

Naturefact
  implement
    instrument
      simple
        removing stick
    weapon
      simple
        missile
        batterer
Artifact
  implement
    instrument
      simple
        removing stick
        food removal cutters
        blade killers
      complex
        grasper
    weapon
      simple
        thrown stunner
        batterer
        hand-held cutter
        thrown impaler
      complex
        projected impaler
        projected stunner
  facility
    tended
      simple
        strangler
        pitfall
        entangler (land, water)
        holder
        hider
        attractor
    untended
      simple
        strangler
        fall
        holder
      complex
        strangler
        moving crusher
        fall

---

agers in general. The net result was that their sustenance could be obtained only through a comparatively narrow range of methods because of the nature of plant growth and animal habits.

Verifying the projections made in opening chapters, the purposes served by natural instruments and weapons were very few in number for the sample societies. The removing sticks, missile stones, and battering clubs are the only natural forms which occurred rather widely. Natural weapons were in fact incapable of effective cutting, as was projected in earlier statements about the qualities of natural forms. Therefore, it is unlikely that men could have been effective hunters using naturefacts alone.

Among the simple instruments identified by functional purpose in Table 7–3, the removal stick served man best to obtain plant food. Occasionally these sticks were supplemented by the use of some form of cutting instrument used to obtain stationary food products. The employment of bladed killers was far more restricted since game usually could escape, making it difficult to bring any form of instrument into effective use. The employment of complex instruments was quite rare, so much so that they must have been largely insignificant on a worldwide basis. The most important conclusions to be drawn about instruments for the sampled societies are that very few types were conceived, these consistently were of simple design, and the elementary developments were logically from naturefacts. In essence it is deduced that an unelaborated technology was sufficient among gatherers for obtaining plant products or confined animals.

Simple artifactual weapons exhibit much more variability as a functional purpose subclass than do their instrumental counterparts. Yet when weapons are considered with care, it becomes apparent that only the hand-held, hand-thrown, or throwing-board projected impalers (spears, leisters, and harpoons) were widely important. Thus, in the sense that the removal stick was critical among instruments, the thrust or thrown impaler was of prime importance among weapons.

In terms of the principles involved, there was greater variability applied to facilities than to implements. Among both tended and untended facilities we find that complex types usually were elaborations on simpler models. Only one complex tended facility was identified for the societies sampled (the Angmagsalik raven-taking snowhouse), but others exist. For example, the Bororo of Brazil, who were foragers, fished with a bag-shaped net which had two pieces of flexible wood attached at right angles to the outer edges of the mouth. The ends of the wooden grips were tied together, and the grips were forced apart, thus opening the net mouth to varying degrees when the form was used (Hay n.d.:53–54).

The evidence presented in this chapter not only tests the taxonomy with respect to empirical findings, but it also provides insights into the evolutionary development of clusters of forms as well as particular types. The conclusions drawn along both dimensions are satisfying in terms of the goals which were outlined at the beginning of the book. It appears further that in assessing the complexity of forms a basic unit for measuring change has been identified. It is not the naturefact or artifact as such, but the number of components or parts which are judged as most important.

EIGHT

The Evolution of Technology

In technology as in all its other aspects, evolution means orderly change through time with the probability that forms will become increasingly complex. The development of human social life, language, and political organization from simple to complex has already been established in outline, although the details remain elusive. For some dimensions of human experience, such as the terms used for designating kin, evolutionary progressions defy identification (Service 1960; Wallace 1961). For others, such as descent systems or marriage forms, progressions clearly are not cumulative (for example, Moore 1954; Wolf 1964). It is, however, accepted that material culture grows increasingly complex through time, and it is my contention that many major and certain minor developments may be plotted with considerable precision.

It is reasoned that after a technological product has been conceived and produced, changes in the form are based on the alteration, addition, or multiplication of specific components. Furthermore, it is of vast importance that the manufactures which could have served as possible archetypes from which later forms developed were very few. Particular changes occur largely as step-by-step attribute modifications, and this makes it possible to plot with considerable precision the elaborations in certain lines of productions. There is a second reason why evolutionary change may be plotted with greater ease for manufactures than for other aspects of culture or society. Many aboriginal hunters around the world made and used some forms which were very simple and also employed others which were comparatively complex. By reducing these manufactures to their components, it becomes possible to compare types reported from anywhere in the world and to make judgments about their comparative

167

development and complexity. In this manner we may begin to recognize the orderly change in material culture. The task may be accomplished rather easily because the principles which led to changes in the past are still being applied in contemporary technological developments. Finally, the taxonomy which has been formulated for the description of subsistants in itself provides insight into lines of evolutionary changes, especially after the inventories of actual hunters have been fitted into the units.

The explicit theme of this study is that culture was derived from a material base most faithfully represented in those forms identified as subsistants. The plan of this chapter is to define the major qualitative changes or "quantum leaps" which took place in this technology. The essence of the changes for all of mankind prior to 10,000 B.C. is outlined as follows:

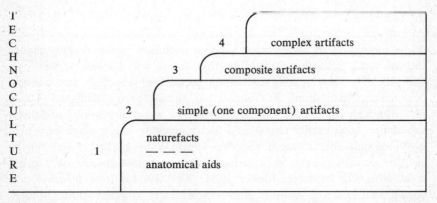

For each technological step the associated material objects are presented in the sections to follow. As a reaction against the labeling of evolutionary levels in culture in terms of social or political organization, and in order to stress all of the points inherent in my approach, I define the levels of cultural evolution only in technological terms.

TECHNOCULTURE 1

Man in genesis obtained his food largely through bodily means. It was *anatomical aids* on which he depended most heavily. These were first supplemented and then vastly enhanced by the use of *naturefacts* which served him throughout this beginning level that is, in certain respects, the "protoculture" stage proposed by A. Irving Hallowell (1956). Man's diet consisted mainly of plant products; he was herbivorous, he browsed, picked, grubbed, and plucked his foods far more often than he slashed and tore, or grabbed and hit to obtain them. This was the "fruit and nuts" subsistence base of savages visualized by Morgan (1877:10) and is the only reasonable beginning admissible. L. B. S. Leakey (1960:57) wrote that at this point in time man "probably, for the most part, . . . lived upon nuts and fruits and upon such things as snails and small rodents, birds' eggs, and fledgeling birds, while he was also, probably, to some extent a scavenger." Leakey (1960 57:66) observed further that given the limited cutting abilities of man's teeth and nails it would be essential for him to have some form of cutting implement before he could tear the hide of an animal of any size in order to consume it. François Bordes (1968:34) takes a similar position: that the first men were most likely scavengers. Loren C. Eiseley (1956:73) writes "since man is really an abnormal carnivore, that his first ventures upon the grass were descents into open parkland in search of seeds, grasshoppers, possibly even wild sorghums, and other items of this sort which could be harvested upon the ground." Eiseley then goes on to note that man's stomach is not that of a true meat eater. The meat sources for emerging man were humble ones, such as insects, reptiles, and small species of game animals, in addition to some large game which was killed by other animals or by accident, or died of old age. It is doubtful that meat could have played a very important part in the diet of elementary man. A recent experiment to obtain meat by running down animals or scavenging in a Tanzanian park with vast game resources, demonstrated that a small group of persons might support themselves in this manner only at certain times of the year and for short intervals (Schaller and Lowther 1969:327).

At the beginnings of this stage men began to employ naturefacts, and the most important form by far was a stick. It might have been long or short, light or heavy, depending on the need of the moment and the forms readily at hand. This simple type was used to dig up roots and tubers, knock down fruit, and batter animals to death. A natural stick was above all else an instrument, for it enabled men to obtain food products incapable of motion. Stones or long bones may have served as instruments to kill an edible but dangerous insect, to crush the shell of a tortoise, or break open the skull of an already dead game animal, but seldom to kill game. Sticks and stones rarely served as weapons in a strict sense because they lacked the capacity to cut and kill in their natural state and therefore could not effectively be used against creatures capable of motion. When a sleeping animal, or an animal trapped in a bog, or one immobile for other reasons, was killed with a naturefact, the usage was as an instrument, not as a weapon, because the animal was incapable of escaping. When did this stage begin? Probably during the Pliocene rather than the Pleistocene.

TECHNOCULTURE 2

This stage did not develop until long after the use of naturefacts, particularly sticks and stones, had become well established as a pattern of learned behavior. The level began and ended with the fashioning of *simple artifacts*, each with a single material component. At this stage it came to be realized for the first time that raw materials which were reduced in size could serve a given purpose better than an unmodified form. This heralded the discovery of the *reduction process* in technology. The most important form by far was a stick straightened and sharpened at one end with one's teeth. This implement prevailed because it served as a more effective digging stick than one which was unmodified. Such a prepared form was carried about by men and women alike because it sometimes could not be made at a moment of need. Foresight and planning were involved in this as in all other technological productions. A sharpened stick was used to dig animals from their burrows and to kill them, as well as to obtain plant foods; thus it served both as an instrument and as a weapon. Small game which had been cornered but was dangerous to grasp by hand was battered or prodded to death. In time a stick was thrown at moving creatures, and at this point a sexual division of artifact usage began. Women used sticks for digging, and men employed similar sticks not only for digging but also to kill animals. Some missile sticks became elongated into the earliest effective spears; it was only after this point had been reached that man could have embarked on a meaningful career as a hunter. Thus it is proposed that hominids did not learn to hunt effectively until after the rise of incipient culture. Sticks probably were modified before stones because of their use with plant products, which were handled most intensively during early food-getting activities. Furthermore, comparatively few forms of stone, such as flint and quartzite, are capable of being chipped to produce sharp edges. Flaked stones served first as tools, as substitutes for human teeth, rather than as hand-held weapons. The reason is that manipulating them by hand could not extend man's reach effectively to cut and wound a large animal. At close range a wounded animal was likely to lunge at and injure or kill the user. A digging-missile stick served man better as a killer of small game. When digging and missile sticks, as well as simple shaft spears, were pointed at one end with stone knives, they became the first extrasomatic production tools. This stage began during the early Pleistocene.

TECHNOCULTURE 3

This level of achievement, which did not take place so very long ago, became a reality when people habitually manufactured *composite artifacts*. It was then that men modified natural materials and combined these into finished forms. The two or more components might be of the same material, as in woven baskets of vines, or of two different materials, as would be the case when a wooden handle was fitted to a stone knife blade. Once materials with different properties were joined as the essential components to finished forms, the possibilities of vast technological changes began to be realized. The idea of binders led to many diverse possibilities, and one of the most important of these was to fashion an effective haft for a weapon point and efficiently attach hooks at the ends of poles for retrieving hard-to-reach plant products. Only after a stone spearpoint was bound securely to a shaft did hunting efficiency improve greatly, not only with respect to the number of species taken, but more importantly because of the expanded opportunities for killing mature big game animals. This was the era, too, during which the use of artifactual facilities expanded broadly. The use of lures, disguises, and game guides came into being. The employment of facilities required considerable planning, foresight, and other studied considerations.

In a very real sense the technological advances made during Techno-culture 3 would never again be equaled, at least not down to the present time, and to my way of thinking this was the only "revolution" ever to occur in the history of technology. Why? There are a number of very cogent reasons. First of all, the *multiplication process* was discovered, and with it man was able to imitate configurations in nature. This truly was a great event among human achievements. It came to be realized that stones could be piled one on top of another to build a hunting blind which was similar to a naturally clustered group of stones behind which a hunter could hide. Brush could be piled in converging lines to guide game, and possibly stone cairns were made as imitations of men for greater effectiveness in hunting. It was at this stage that the *duplication process*—a refinement of the multiplication process—was discovered, which led to the weaving of containers and the use of multiple but similar points at the ends of weapon shafts. Even more important, at least in certain respects, was the discovery at this time of the *conjunctive principle*, which was essential for the manufacture of composite artifacts. This in turn led to *amplifications in craft mediums*, meaning greater experimentations in working stone, wood, or bone, which produced *design amplifications*.

TECHNOCULTURE 4

This stage of development was attained when *complex artifacts*, those with components which moved when the form was brought into play, were made habitually, a point reached only a short while ago in terms of cultural evolution. Among weapons the most outstanding innovation was the bow and arrow. Unlike any earlier weapon an arrow shot from a bow could be back-sighted for very accurate aim. Furthermore, an arrow speeds through the air as much as three times as fast as a spear thrown by hand, and it will travel twice as far as a spear hurled with the aid of a throwing-board (Semenov 1964:204). The harpoon was also an important complex weapon. It emerged first as the harpoon dart, and from it the toggle-headed type developed. Among facilities, untended sets, represented by the spring-pole snare and various types of deadfalls, were among the most notable achievements.

The earliest complex weapon, however, was the spear and throwing-board in combination; this possibly was invented before the bow was used with effective arrows. Harpoons emerged and were elaborated only after efficient watercraft had been developed. In terms of nonsubsistants, the most important forms were tools which utilized the principle of rotary motion as reflected in the strap, bow, and pump drills. It is needless to elaborate on this level, because all of the peoples discussed previously, except for the Tasmanians, are broadly representative of sub-levels within Technoculture 4.

All that was to be accomplished within the technology of hunters was achieved during Technoculture 4. After this time farming and pastoral economies arose, introducing technological changes of a very different nature from those identified in preceding levels. In order to avoid any misunderstandings about the four levels of technology which I have proposed, a number of very explicit elaborations are required.

I have defined the technological sequence of major changes for culture, not for any particular culture. This is an attempt to plot *the* general evolution or *the* cultural history of technology. Thus, it is not implied that all peoples passed through the same levels or remained in each level for a similar length of time. It is implied, however, that each distinct technological tradition which is represented in the taxonomy followed the same general sequence of developments.

In the statements about the levels of technoculture I have not referred to the clusters of forms represented among any of the peoples discussed in Chapters 3 through 6, except in the closing sentence. I have not suggested nor implied that the Seri represent one particular level and the Caribou Eskimos, or some other people, another level. Why? Because each people, with the probable exception of the Tasmanians, belonged to the most advanced level, Technoculture 4. Then why did I bother to describe the subsistants of the twelve chosen people in such detail? It was only after all the forms which they used were studied, classified, and compared that insight was gained into the logical progression which led from one level to the next and which made possible the comprehension to formulate the technocultures.

In the preface and throughout each chapter it has been argued that man became what he is because of technology. Now is the time to retreat from this forceful position, which is a thesis-in-reaction to other equally forceful one-cause explanations for man's development. Possibly Service is correct in arguing that there is no "prime-mover" in cultural evolution. He writes, "If technology is the prime-mover, then it ought to be useful in explaining the evolution of actual specific societies" (Service 1968: 405). At present this is not possible in terms of the taxonomy which I have advanced. Service goes on to write:

> To be sure, some kind of technological production of necessities, especially of food, is required for any society. In the context of evolution, such production is an enabler, so to speak, without which an increase in size and density could not take place. But a necessity or enabler is not necessarily a mover. Many stabilized societies could produce much more than they do, but it does not follow that they necessarily will, nor that if they did that they would necessarily "evolve" in some sense (Service 1968: 406–407).

In this general context I have not isolated a prime-mover but rather offer a more adequate understanding about the development of technological enablers among hunters.

I must retreat from the thesis of the omnipotence of technology in other directions as well. Had man's social life been organized differently, say with the primary bonds between siblings, then technological knowledge probably would have accreted in a different manner than that which we presume. Technology would have developed differently also if man's biological qualities contrasted with those which we recognize as so very human. If our vision were different, our forearms shorter, the digits on each hand numbered three rather than five, if we had no opposable thumb, developments in technology would be quite different from those with which we are familiar. Similarly, there is a moral quality in human thinking which guides the use of manufactures. Man does not covet all the products of technology, and often social, political, or religious norms negate technological accomplishments. As Loren C. Eiseley (1956:68) has observed, man "lives on dreams and is in that sense unique. It is not the ax in the hand but the symbols flowing through the time tracts in the head that are the real tools of this creature." In order not to leave the impression that I have abandoned the very essence of my thesis, I offer a final quotation from Leslie A. White (1949:366), "We are now in possession of a key to an understanding of the growth and development of culture: technology."

CONJECTURAL SCHEME FOR SUBSISTANT EVOLUTION

The words "conjectural scheme" are to be interpreted literally since my purpose at the moment is to speculate about the trend toward increasing complexity among subsistants in the virtual absence of paleoethno-graphic evidence. The rationale for the relative placement of types is offered insofar as possible, but admittedly some of the reasons are quite weak. Anti-evolutionists will find this section to be especially appalling. I will be accused of having assumed that which I have set out to prove, and nowhere is this strategy more apparent than in the paragraphs to follow. In a sense I admit that it is so, but given the completeness of the evidence from excavations and a focal interest in technology, I know of no reasonable option except to speculate in the most logical manner possi-ble. In Tables 8–1 and 8–2 developmental sequences for the emergence of most subsistants are offered. The ordering within a circle is more meaning-ful than the relationship of one cluster to another. In chronological terms it is implied that forms occurring lower on the tables were originated before those which are at a higher level.

Table 8–1   A hypothesized developmental sequence for artifactual implements.

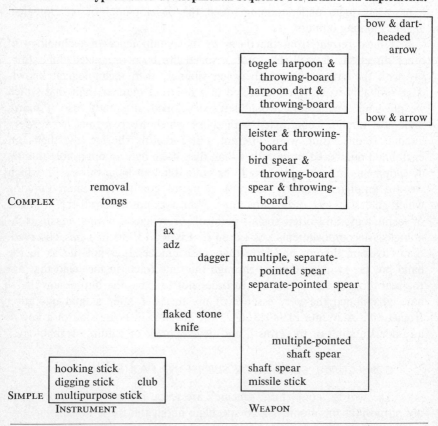

In the text it has been suggested repeatedly that a stick used for multiple food-getting purposes was the archetype for implements. Its possible uses included digging, dislodging, battering, probing, hurling, and piercing in order to obtain edibles. Above all else, this instrument performed certain tasks more effectively than did human fingernails, hands, and arms. From it was developed the earliest specialized instrument, the digging stick, designed to remove edibles from the ground. A heavy stick became a club, and if a long, light stick were hooked at the end it served to remove inaccessible edibles from plants. The digging stick was the only type which remained of long-term and critical importance through much of the evolution of technology. It not only served foragers as their primary means for digging up plant and animal foods, but it was the key instrument for cultivating the soil among small-scale farmers. Minor modifications were made in a number of different societies, but the form was not widely displaced until after the invention of the plow.

Cutting tools were used mainly to process raw materials in the manu-

Table 8–2   A hypothesized developmental sequence for artifactual facilities.

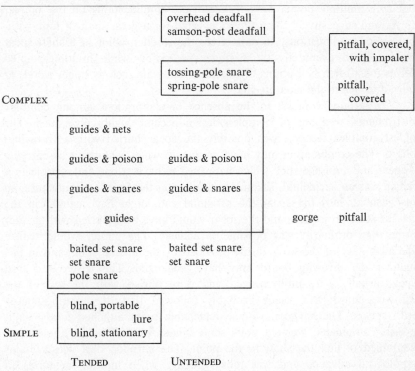

	TENDED	UNTENDED		
	overhead deadfall samson-post deadfall			pitfall, covered, with impaler
	tossing-pole snare spring-pole snare			pitfall, covered
COMPLEX				
	guides & nets			
	guides & poison	guides & poison		
	guides & snares	guides & snares		
	guides		gorge pitfall	
	baited set snare set snare pole snare	baited set snare set snare		
	blind, portable lure blind, stationary			
SIMPLE				

facture of artifacts. Although knives, adzes, and axes served to obtain food products on occasion, this use probably was not of great importance. If foods which had to be cut from their source were widely important, we would expect to find specialized food-obtaining cutters, but these are rare among foragers. The dagger is such a specialized form in a sense, but it probably was used most often to kill an animal already wounded by a weapon or confined by a facility. The same would apply to other cutting instruments employed against creatures incapable of motion, such as an awl for killing captured fish.

Removal tongs were the most widely-occurring complex instrument, but even they were not common. Suggestively, the employment of a mechanical principle in an instrumental manner to obtain food was of comparatively recent origin and was largely unimportant on a world-wide basis.

Presumably the multipurpose stick was the prototype for the club, digging and missile stick, and the simple shaft spear. Each was a stick of a different length or weight, and most were sharpened at one end. The elongated missile stick became a simple shaft spear, and the latter was the archetype for weapons. Possibly spears made from one piece of wood but with multiple points were technological amplifications on the simpler form, and suggestively these types persisted for a great span of time without major modifications. In most areas the wooden point of a shaft spear was replaced eventually by a stone spearpoint, while multiple-pointed forms most often had points of nonlithic materials such as bone, wood, or horn attached to the separate shaft.

In striking contrast to the absence of elaborations among complex instruments, weapons of complex design became highly diversified. The oldest complex weapon was possibly the spear hurled with a throwing-board. The combination may have originated when a hunter was carrying a spear and a missile stick which happened to have at one end a projection which was an accidental, secondary product in the form's manufacture. In his haste to hurl the spear the proximal end might have caught in the missile stick projection, and the spear would have been hurled with greater force than ordinarily was possible to achieve. The hunter would realize the advantage of the extra thrust provided by the missile stick, and in this manner the throwing-board may have originated. The leister and bird spear usually were multipronged and were hurled with the aid of the throwing-board; this usage probably followed that of throwing-boards with spears. The harpoon with a detachable point attached to the shaft possibly originated when a point-shaft binder worked its way loose but continued to link the shaft to the point. The harpoon dart was a major typological advance and was most effective when hunting creatures in water. It probably did not become elaborated until after effective water-craft had developed. The toggle-headed harpoon is simply a further elaboration on the harpoon dart.

A reasonably direct evolutionary line leads from the simple shaft spear to the toggle-headed harpoon used with the throwing-board. The origination of the bow and arrow, however, is a separate development and one of the most striking of all abrupt innovations in the development of weaponry among hunters. In all likelihood it was a toy long before emerging as an effective hunting implement. Its elaborations are well known, and the apex of these among foragers is the dart-headed arrow. This form is an arrow pointed with a harpoon dart rather than an arrowpoint.

It is reasoned that the earliest tended sets (Table 8–2) were stationary hunting blinds made from stones, branches, or brush, and that these were modeled after natural blinds. In time an animal might have been lured near a blind by placing one of its favored foods near the spot where a hunter was concealed. Portable blinds made by attaching branches to a hunter's body may have been an early development from the stationary blind. A snare attached to the end of a hand-held pole possibly was the earliest type of direct game-holding facility, and again when bait was placed nearby to lure an animal, the form was likely to function in a more effective manner. The next step might have been to set a snare which did not require tending and to bait it. For some species it was necessary to tend a set snare because certain animals had the capacity to break free shortly after they were captured.

Game guides made of brush or branches were in all likelihood a comparatively early development, and these originally were used in conjunction with weapons. In time openings were left in guide fences, and these were hung with snares, tended or untended, depending on the nature of the game. The use of such guides became even more refined once poisons were used in conjunction with them. Further refinements emerged when guides were used with nets. Parenthetically, it should be noted that in this conjectured sequence of originations, cooperation in hunting emerged by slow steps.

Among simple untended sets the gorge possibly had considerable antiquity, and a simple pitfall may likewise be a facility invented long ago. Among untended sets, the spring- and tossing-pole types of snares are the most direct developments from simple to complex, and this also is true of complex pitfalls. Complex tended sets were represented in the societies sampled only by the Angmagsalik raven snowhouse trap. The most novel form of facility, which cannot by definition be simple, is the deadfall, and according to the scheme of changes which has been purported, deadfalls must be innovations of comparatively recent origins.

In the evolutionary development of subsistant usages it is presumed that human skill, cunning, and persistence were constants in the employment of forms. Ethnographic evidence for the twelve sampled societies and a casual survey of writings about other foragers suggest that rituals were integrated with only a few subsistant usages. Possibly this had been true for a long span of time. It was reasonably common for aboriginal foragers to perform magic before a hunt, especially if the quarry was expected to be elusive or dangerous. It was less common, but by no means rare, for people to perform propitiation rituals after kills had been made or harvests reaped. Persons in search of food often carried charms or amulets, and particular behavior might be expected of family members who remained at home. Yet formulas or other forms of magic were seldom involved in the actual procurement of food. One example to the contrary occurs among the Nomlaki of California. Considerable danger was involved when trees were climbed in order to obtain pine cones. This was the only vegetable food harvested by the men, and those who did so were specialists. They employed one long, hooked pole as a tree-climbing aid and another shorter one to dislodge the pine cones. As a man climbed a tree, another at the foot of it chanted and kept time with his foot, apparently a ritual designed to protect the climber (Goldschmidt 1951:410).

PALEOETHNOGRAPHIC RECORD FOR SUBSISTANT ORIGINS

The subsistant taxonomy, as presented in Table 2–1, was designed to reflect the logical development of forms through time. Thus it has been reasoned that naturefacts were employed before artifacts were made, that implements were conceived before facilities, that instruments originated earlier than weapons, and so on. The most reasonable test for the logic of the sequence is to plot it against paleoethnographic recoveries from excavations. Unfortunately we may anticipate comparatively few rewards from such an effort. Many subsistants were made entirely from organic materials, which are rarely preserved for great spans of time. Then too some manufactures have been recovered only in very fragmentary condition, which makes it difficult if not impossible to establish their intended purpose. Finally, the oldest preserved artifacts usually are made of stone, but the functions of some of these forms are conjectured.

The first question is: Have we any evidence for a clear naturefact stage in the paleoethnographic record? The answer is no; if one did exist, it probably would not be recognized as such unless the materials were in very intimate association with hominid remains. Even if battered stones were found in a level with human bones, it would be difficult to prove that the marks were made from usage by man rather than from natural causes. The naturefact stage is and possibly long will be conjectural.

The next question is: Have naturefacts been found in direct association with hominid remains and simple artifacts? If so then a pure naturefact stage might have logical credibility. The most important finds in this
regard were recovered by Raymond A. Dart at Makapansgat in South
Africa. Here the remains of australopithecines are associated with certain
animal bones used as naturefacts and others which had been fashioned
into artifacts. This is a clear step above and beyond a pure naturefact
stage. Once hominids had become reasonably effective hunters of adult
species of large animals, we would expect them to have developed extrasomatic means for dismembering the kills. We might conjecture too that
the intact bones of slain animals would have served as naturefacts and
that some bones would be modified to function as artifacts. Possibly the
first artifacts were made of bone and were produced as a secondary result
of butchering techniques. It appears that just such developments may
have given rise to the osteodontokeratic (bone, tooth, and horn) culture
remains at Makapansgat. Here antelope long bones were used as clubs to
kill baboons. These serve as the clearest example of a naturefact subsistant type. Furthermore, horns were used as picks, toothed jaws as cutters,
and pelvic bones as well as shoulder blades served as chopping tools.
Some artifacts were produced by splitting bones, and other bone frag-
ments were trimmed secondarily; these types include daggers, knife-like
blades, gouge-like tools, and short sections of one bone inserted into another with the condyles missing from both bones (Dart 1957:1960). The
validity of these finds has not been questioned, but the interpretation of
them as cultural remains is open to debate. Yet the tendency is to accept
at least the use of antelope long bones as baboon-killing clubs. Given the
sequence for the evolution of manufacturing methods that I have proposed,
I would presume that a cultural stage in which naturefacts and very simple artifacts occur together must have existed. Whether the combination
did in fact occur at Makapansgat, I am not in a position to determine.
Before passing on to evidence from elsewhere, however, two additional
points must be offered concerning these South African finds. Presumably
the cannon bones (one bone inserted into another with the condyles broken
from each) were tools of a composite form. It might appear that the
presence of this type would invalidate my proposal that one-component
artifacts were made before composite types. I would presume that the
bone-working at Makapansgat is an advanced technological development
which was preceded by an earlier, simpler stage in which only one-
component artifacts were produced. The final point is that the worked
bone represented by these finds appears to have died off with the
australopithecines and thus represents a deadend genesis of culture (for
example, Wolberg 1970).

Not only is it debated whether the australopithecines actually produced artifacts of bone, but there is also the problem of distinguishing between stones whose fractures were produced naturally as opposed to those made by man. Lower Paleolithic recoveries from a number of areas in the Old World include flaked stones which cannot be ascribed clearly either to human production or to formation by natural forces. Included in this category would be Kafuan forms best known from finds in Uganda, the pre-Chellean stones of East Anglia, and the Cromer flakes, also from England (for example, Leakey 1960:66–68). These finds represent a logical beginning for stone tool production, but whether the examples cited were made by man is unclear. One authority on the subject, Grahame Clark (1969:27), regards the Cromerian flakes as the product of wave action and the Kafuan stones as flaked by rapids and waterfalls in gorges. Yet François Bordes (1968:45) accepts the possibility that natural stones were used before those which were fashioned purposefully, and this is a generally accepted stance. If this position is valid, then the Kafuan, pre-Chellean, and Cromer forms could represent the first step in stone tool utilization. It is also possible that they were altered by natural means and then utilized by hominids.

Paleoethnographers usually have regarded emerging man as omnivorous (for example, Clark 1969:32) and judged that he soon became an efficient hunter. Evidence to support this thesis rests in part with the preponderance of bones from small game and immature animals of larger species in some early sites. Following this early evidence there is a rapid increase in the number of bones from adult animals of large species. The presumption is that this indicates an emergent hunting efficiency, although it is difficult to determine the number of hunters who contributed to a particular bone pile or the span of time over which the bones at one particular level in a site accumulated. The simple shaft spear is presumed to have been one of the earliest effective weapons. The head of one such spear was found from the Clactonian in England (Bordes 1968:95) and possibly dates about 400,000 years ago. In addition the upper section of a wooden shaft with a fire-hardened tip was recovered from among the rib remains of an elephant at Lehringen near Verden, Germany (Clark 1969: 41). This spear dates from the Riss-Wurm interglacial.

Recent finds in Kenya include core tools, such as choppers, dating 2.6 million years ago, and in the Lower Omo Valley of Ethiopia stone artifacts have been recovered which are nearly three million years old (Isaac et al. 1971). It truly is remarkable that for over two million years the changes in stone artifacts were primarily variations around a small number of stable types such as choppers and hand axes. Composite forms do not appear to have been manufactured until comparatively recent times. For the Old World Paleolithic bolas often are isolated as the first composite forms; if the identification is correct, they would be the first "complex" subsistant type. Bolas are ascribed to the Chellean-Acheulean of Africa and Portugal by Leakey (1960:81) and presumably to the Mousterian by Clark (1969:44). The identification of stones as bola balls is based largely on their recovery in sets of threes. Presumably each stone was tied to a thong, and these were bound together at their distal ends. (I cannot but recall repeatedly finding natural spherical stones in clusters of threes in a Western Eskimo site. I thought that they had been for bolas until an Eskimo woman picked up three stones and began juggling them, saying that such was their purpose.) S. A. Semenov (1964:201–203) in a very detailed study of the forms and wear patterns of Paleolithic artifacts states that none of the Neanderthalian (Mousterian) stone tools had separate handles. He also rejects the identification of round stones as bolas for this period. Furthermore, Semenov attributes the manufacture of composite tools to the upper Paleolithic and asserts that their systematic production did not occur until the Mesolithic. If this is so, then it becomes difficult to accept the existence of bolas in the mid-Paleolithic or earlier times.

Comparatively little agreement exists concerning when the earliest stone spearpoints appeared. Leakey (1960:100–101) attributes them to the Sangoan of Africa which dates about 80,000 years ago, while Bordes (1968:138) comments that they are rare as late as the middle Paleolithic which ended some 37,000 years ago. Clark (1969) in *World Prehistory* does not mention them until Mesolithic times! From appearances it would seem that some of the large chipped stone blades from Mousterian times onward could have been effective spearpoints. It is difficult to imagine that some of the tanged stone points of varying sizes which appear during the Solutrean were not used to head spears. In France by the early Aurignacian, some 29,000 years ago, conical, bone spearpoints with split bases were recovered, but this haft soon was abandoned in favor of a variety with a single bevel, which continued to be popular into the Magdalenian beginning about 17,000 years age (Bordes 1968: 155, 163).

The bow and arrow possibly originated in Africa near the end of the Paleolithic, some 17,000 years ago. In Africa lunate blades may have been set in the sides of arrowheads during the Capsian (Cole 1963:261–262). In Europe during the middle stages of the Magdalenian, the throwing-board was used, but it seemingly was displaced by the bow and arrow about 14,000 years ago (Bordes 1968:164, 238).

The harpoon dart is first found in the middle stages of the Magdalenian in Europe, about 13,000 years ago. Made from bone, the early varieties were barbed on one side only, while later examples had barbs on opposite sides. In the succeeding Azilian period, about 9000 years ago, a line hole was drilled into the base just above the tang of bilaterally barbed harpoon darts made from antler (Bordes 1968:164–166). It does not seem that the toggle-headed harpoon used by Eskimos was derived from the harpoon dart of the late Paleolithic or Mesolithic in Europe. Admittedly some toggling harpoon heads have been found in northern Scandinavia (for example, Gjessing 1944:16–18), but the Eskimo type more likely was originated from the harpoon dart used by maritime hunters in eastern Asia. The reason for not attributing the toggle harpoon of northern Europe and that of northern North America to a common origin is that it is not reported between the Kolyma River in Siberia and Scandinavia (Rudenko 1961:175–176).

As inadequate as the paleoethnographic record may be, it does provide a broad scale test for the ordering of units in the subsistant taxonomy which has been advanced. It certainly seems that simple, one-component types were used for most of cultural time and that not until the early phases of the Upper Paleolithic did men begin to fashion composite artifacts. With the possible exception of bolas, complex subsistants were not originated until the close of the Paleolithic or even later.

CLOSING COMMENTS

This work is an appeal for anthropologists to consider the manufactures of peoples systematically in their comparative and evolutionary studies of culture. That someone would write a book along the lines of this one in the 1970s was quite predictable given the renaissance of evolutionary studies in anthropology and our cultural concern in the United States with technology. The formulation of evolutionary classifications by anthropologists since World War II began when Carleton S. Coon (1948) spelled out "levels of cultural complexity" on the basis of institutional relationships. This bold pioneering effort was followed by the formulation of an evolutionary framework on the basis of "community patterning" by Richard K. Beardsley et al. (1956). More recently Service (1962) chose social organization as the basis for his presentation of long-term changes in human behavior. Yet no one since the turn of the century has sought to establish a detailed sequence of evolutionary developments in technology. Why? Possibly because a major effort along these lines by Lewis H. Morgan (1877) was exposed as factually inadequate and conceptually inconsistent. Possibly the cultural materialism of Karl Marx made the subject taboo to some, or perhaps it was simply because studies of material culture were no longer stylish. There are, of course, other reasons why broad scale studies of technology through time have not been attempted. One is that many anthropologists in the recent past, especially members of the Boasian school, felt that their primary mission was to record ethnographic details about vanishing aboriginal cultures before such information was forever lost. Other persons, such as Clark Wissler, expended a great deal of energy assembling and plotting aboriginal base-line data on a continent-wide basis to develop the culture area concept. Still others focused on the diffusion of traits or complexes, or the independent origins of ideas leading to the production of similar styles in artifacts. Yet these (for example, Mason 1966; Sayce 1965) and additional concerns with material culture have served only as a faded backdrop to most anthropological interests.

Within the broad scope of anthropology, it is only those investigators concerned with excavated cultural leavings, paleoethnographers, who have advanced the study of manufactures through time to a significant degree. Yet it is my contention that the detailed analysis of ethnographic collections in museums would offer far greater potential for understanding the evolution of technology than all of the excavated recoveries combined. There is clear irony in the fact that even with the severe limitations inherent in paleoethnographic methodology, it is these investigators, not museum curators, who have contributed the most knowledge about the development of technology. Ethnographic museums, with their potential for being great centers of learning, have become intellectual tombs.

In this and all the other chapters I have drawn narrow- and broad-range conclusions in many different contexts, and I have nothing really new to offer in the way of interpretations at this point. At the same time I am fully aware that the data presented embody many lines of inquiry which I have chosen not to pursue for a multitude of reasons. I find it fitting to close this book by suggesting some of the ways in which the taxonomy, cultural data, and the notions about evolution in technology might profitably be applied.

I have no firm conviction that my sample societies are representative of the major climatic zones with which they are associated; this is true especially for foragers in temperate regions. Such an admission is an open invitation for others to analyze data for different groups of foragers by geographical area. It also would be rewarding to evaluate the subsistant technologies for many groups of hunters who occupied a unified landmass, such as Australia, with different climatic zones. This enterprise would be another test of the extent of differences stimulated by the environment. Studies of this nature would make it possible to accept or reject the interim conclusions which I have drawn about the occurrence of subsistant types, numbers, and components within different habitats.

In the text the social interaction necessary for the employment of subsistants has been mentioned only in passing. This critical dimension to food-getting efforts invites systematic analysis and was ignored in this study only in an effort to stress technology. By plotting the roles of human performers and counting the numbers of individuals involved, the social dimensions of subsistant usages could be revealed. Quite clearly certain instruments, weapons, and sets could not be manipulated by one man or even by a small number of persons. By calculating the individuals required for the effective employment of subsistant clusters, considerable insight would be gained into the nature of task groups, cooperative activities, and patterns of leadership. Such an endeavor should also contribute to an understanding of socio-subsistant evolution.

For the sample societies only aboriginal base-line data have been considered in the analysis. In terms of technological acculturation among aboriginal peoples, it would be very inviting to assess the changing subsistant technologies of foragers in different areas of the world as they were exposed increasingly to contact with Euro-Americans. The nature of certain changes is obvious, such as the adoption of firearms, but what about the employment of facilities and aids? Surely there is a widescale patterning in the nature of responses. Nonadaptive assimilations would be revealed also, contributing to an increased understanding of acculturative failures. In addition this type of study might provide a sequence for the abandonment of certain technological forms. For example, field-work (1970–1971) among Eskimos of western Alaska has led me to the realization that the aboriginal forms retained longer than any others usually have only one or two components.

We know that by the time ethnographers described many hunters, their ways of life had already changed profoundly from aboriginal times. Many superficial changes are obvious and may be accounted for without difficulty. Yet changes of a greater magnitude are often involved, and these frequently defy ready identification. It seems that the absence or virtual absence of facilities among certain peoples reflects some major cultural upheaval before they were described. For example, the Siriono (Holmberg 1950) and some of the Kaingang (Henry 1941) probably were farmers in fully aboriginal times, but when described they depended either entirely (Kaingang) or almost entirely (Siriono) on foraging activities for food. Neither utilized facilities. Something dramatic was changing the Seri way of life when they were first described, and they had no facilities. Among some of the Ituri Pygmies (Turnbull 1965) one facility was important, the game net, but they used no others. Suggestively the absence or scarcity of facilities is a possible index to other changes.

Along yet another tack, the component analysis which has been offered invites comparative tests to determine its possible validity. I have presumed that once a new form was conceived, it changed significantly in form either through the addition or multiplication of components. This assumption could be tested by a detailed analysis such as was made of leisters from Poland (Znamierowska-Pruffer 1966) and could be carried out for the toggle-headed harpoon complex among Eskimos (Bandi 1969), or many other forms.

Only scattered references have been made concerning the implications of the taxonomy for paleoethnographers and paleoethnologists. Yet it seems to me that some of the ideas which have been put forth merit consideration by such persons. For example, if one anticipated excavating a seventeenth-century Chumash site in California, it would be quite reasonable first to study the ethnographic record and from it plot the subsistant forms and determine those components which one might expect to be preserved. I realize that this approach could be taken without recourse to the taxonomy which has been advanced, but the clear identification of subsistants might add a valuable dimension. Even more appealing would be the determination of key artifacts which would serve as "index components." Obvious examples are spearpoints, which indicate the existence of simple weapons, and arrow-points, which are indicators of a complex form. This task would be made difficult by the fact that most key components would not likely be preserved.

Nowhere in the taxonomy have I attempted to analyze the specific techniques involved when components were joined. Among the obvious examples are pegging, socketing, and scarfing. Once again the number of means for combining components seems limited to variations around a small number of possibilities. By exploring this dimension the limitations of technological knowledge among foragers would be established along yet another tangent.

Another appealing possibility would be to test the usefulness of the concept "tribe" by making subsistant comparisons. We presume that the bands of a tribe are essentially homogeneous in terms of their manufactures; yet in fact, we are able to cite any number of exceptions. It would be more than a term paper exercise to assemble the data about subsistants for the bands of tribes in different areas of the world (possibly the Pomo of California and the Kutchin of northern Alaska and Canada). I suspect that the presumption of tribal units, at least in terms of their subsistants, is invalid. As an extension of this proposal, the subsistants of the above peoples, or others, might be compared with those of adjacent and closely related tribes to establish degrees of regional variability. I suspect that the conclusions drawn from such studies would be revealing, especially if they were correlated with ecological factors.

Possibly the most inviting of all directions in which to expand on the taxonomic base would be to consider the subsistants of food producers, those peoples with pastoral and farming economies. It appears that in their technologies instruments and tended facilities dominate and expand with increasing productivity. At the same time untended sets and weapons decline steadily in importance. Yet soon after a people become food producers, the diversity of weapons and untended sets appears to increase over the number of forms found among foragers in the same climatic zones. As food production expands, the category of natural aids becomes increasingly important and is supplemented by the use of tended facilities. It is my feeling that the essence of the taxonomy, as it has been formulated for the food-getting forms among hunters, may be expanded to include the farming equipment of peoples such as the aboriginal Hopi in Arizona, the Araucanians of Chile, and farming corporations as they exist currently in the Imperial Valley of California.

The foundation for all human lifeways is economic, and for over three million years people have used naturefacts and artifacts in order to build and sustain their patterns in culture. Innumerable postulates, hypotheses, theories, and models have been advanced to explain changes in food-getting networks. Most offer only casual, if not cursory, comments about the details of the technologies employed. The theme of this study is that changes in subsistence patterns are based largely on the innovation of technological particulars. It is suggested further that knowledge about long- and short-term changes in essential technology is most fruitfully achieved through the detailed analysis of the actual forms which men have used and made in order to obtain food.

Bibliography

Anell, Bengt, 1960, "Hunting and Trapping Methods in Australia and Oceania," *Studia Ethnographica Upsaliensia*, vol. 18.

Bandi, Hans-Georg, 1969, *Eskimo Prehistory*. College, Alaska: University of Alaska Press.

Basedow, Herbert, 1925, *Australian Aboriginal*. Adelaide, Australia: F. W. Peece and Sons.

Beaglehole, John C., ed., 1955, *Journals of Captain James Cook on His Voyages of Discovery*, vol. 1. Cambridge, England: Hakluyt Society.

Beardsley, Richard K., et al., 1956, "Functional and Evolutionary Implications of Community Patterning," in *Seminars in Archaeology: 1955*, Robert Wauchope, ed. Society for American Archaeology Memoir No. 11, pp. 129–157.

Beatty, Harry, 1951, "A Note on the Behavior of the Chimpanzee," *Journal of Mammalogy* 32:118.

Birket-Smith, Kaj, 1929, "The Caribou Eskimos," *Report of the Fifth Thule Expedition 1921–4*, vol. 5, pts. 1, 2.

Bleek, Dorothea F., 1928, *Naron*. Cambridge, England: Cambridge University Press.

Bordes, François, 1968, *Old Stone Age*. New York: McGraw-Hill, Inc.

Braidwood, Robert J., 1963, *Prehistoric Men*. Chicago: Chicago Natural History Museum.

Bunzel, Ruth, 1938, "Art," in *General Anthropology*, Franz Boas, ed. New York: D. C. Heath and Company, pp. 535–588.

Carpenter, C. R., 1934, "A Field Study of the Behavior and Social Relations of Howling Monkeys," *Comparative Psychology Monographs*, vol. 10, no. 2.

———, 1935, "Behavior of Red Spider Monkeys in Panama," *Journal of Mammalogy* 16:171–180.

Chisholm, A. H., 1954, "The Use by Birds of 'Tools' or 'Instruments,'" *Ibis* 96:380–383.

187

Clark, Grahame, 1969, *World Prehistory*. Cambridge, England: Cambridge University Press.

Cole, Sonia, 1963, *Prehistory of East Africa*. New York: The Macmillan Company.

Coon, Carleton S., 1948, *A Reader in General Anthropology*. New York: Holt, Rinehart and Winston, Inc.

Dart, Raymond A., 1957, "The Osteodontokeratic Culture of Australopithecus Prometheus," *Transvaal Museum Memoir* no. 10.

————, 1960, "The Bone Tool-manufacturing Ability of Australopithecus Prometheus," *American Anthropologist*, n.s., 62:134–143.

Dunn, E. J., 1931, *Bushmen*. London: Charles Griffin & Co., Ltd.

Eiseley, Loren C., 1956, "Fossil Man and Human Evolution," in *Yearbook of Anthropology—1955*, William L. Thomas, Jr., ed. Chicago: University of Chicago Press, pp. 61–78.

Elkin, A. P., 1964, *Australian Aborigines*. New York: Doubleday & Company, Inc.

Fisher, Edna M., 1939, "Habits of the Southern Sea Otter," *Journal of Mammalogy* 20:21–36.

Fürer-Haimendorf, Christoph von, 1943, "The Chenchus," in *Aboriginal Tribes of Hyderabad*, vol. 1. London: Macmillan & Co., Ltd.

Gjessing, Gutorm, 1944, "Circumpolar Stone Age," *Acta Arctica*, vol. 2.

Goldschmidt, Walter, 1951, "Nomlaki Ethnography," *University of California Publications in American Archaeology and Ethnology*, vol. 42, pt. 4.

Goodall, Jane, 1965, "Chimpanzees of the Gombe Stream Reserve," in *Primate Behavior*, Irven DeVore, ed. New York: Holt, Rinehart and Winston, Inc., pp. 425–473.

————, 1968, "Tool-using Bird: The Egyptian Vulture," *National Geographic* 133:630–641.

Gould, Richard A., 1969, *Yiwara: Foragers of the Australian Desert*. New York: Charles Scribner's Sons.

Gusinde, Martin, 1961, *Yamana*. 5 vols. New Haven, Conn.: Human Relations Area Files.

Hall, K. R. L., 1968, "Tool-using Performances as Indicators of Behavioral Adaptability," in *Primates*, Phyllis C. Jay, ed. New York: Holt, Rinehart and Winston, Inc., pp. 131–148.

————, and Schaller, George B., 1964, "Tool-using Behavior of the California Sea Otter," *Journal of Mammalogy* 45:287–298.

Hallowell, A. Irving, 1956, "The Structural and Functional Dimensions of a Human Existence," *Quarterly Review of Biology* 31:88–101.

Hay, Alex. R., n.d., *Saints and Savages*. London: Hodder & Stoughton, Ltd.

Henry, Jules, 1941, *Jungle People*. Richmond, Va.: J. J. Augustin, Inc.

Holmberg, Allan R., 1950, "Nomads of the Long Bow," *Smithsonian Institution, Institute of Social Anthropology Publ.* no. 10.

Honigmann, John J., 1959, *World of Man*. New York: Harper & Row, Publishers.

Horne, G., and Aiston, G., 1924, *Savage Life in Central Australia*. London: Macmillan & Co., Ltd.

Hyades, P., and Deniker, J., 1891, *Mission Scientifique du Cap Horn*. Paris: Gautier-Villars et Fils.

Isaac, Glynn L., et al., 1971, "Archeological Traces of Early Hominid Activities, East of Lake Rudolf, Kenya," *Science* 173:1129–1133.

Jay, Phyllis C., 1968, "Primate Field Studies and Human Evolution," in *Primates*, Phyllis C. Jay, ed. New York: Holt, Rinehart and Winston, Inc., pp. 487–503.

Kroeber, Alfred L., 1931, "The Seri," *Southwest Museum Papers*, no. 6.

Lancaster, Jane B., 1968, "On the Evolution of Tool-using Behavior," *American Anthropologist*, n.s., 70:56–66.

Leakey, L. B. S., 1960, *Adam's Ancestors*. New York: Harper & Row, Publishers.

Lee, Richard B., 1966, "Subsistence Ecology of Kung Bushmen." Ph.D. dissertation, University of California, Berkeley, 1965.

Lowie, Robert H., 1937, *History of Ethnological Theory*. New York: Rinehart & Co., Inc.

McConnel, Ursula H., 1953–1955, "Native Arts and Industries on the Archer, Kendall and Holroyd Rivers, Cape York Peninsula, North Queensland," *Records of the South Australia Museum* 11:1–42.

McGee, W J, 1898, "The Seri Indians," *Seventeenth Annual Report of the Bureau of American Ethnology, 1895–96*, pt. 1, 1–344.

McKennan, Robert A., 1959, "The Upper Tanana Indians," *Yale University Publications in Anthropology*, no. 55.

Man, Edward H., 1882, "On the Andamanese and Nicobarese Objects Presented to Maj.-Gen. Pitt Rivers, F.R.S.," *Journal of the Anthropological Institute of Great Britain and Ireland* 11:268–291.

———, 1883, "On the Aboriginal Inhabitants of the Andaman Islands," *Journal of the Anthropological Institute of Great Britain and Ireland* 12:69–116, 117–175, 327–434.

Marshall, A. J., 1960, "Bower-birds," *Endeavour* 19:202–208.

Mason, Otis T., 1966, *Origins of Invention*. Cambridge, Mass.: M.I.T. Press (originally published in 1895).

Meggitt, M. J., 1965, "The Association between Australian Aborigines and Dingoes," in *Man, Culture, and Animals*, Anthony Leeds and Andrew P. Vayda, eds. Washington, D.C.: American Association for the Advancement of Science, pp. 7–26.

Merfield, Fred G., and Miller, Harry, 1956, *Gorillas Were My Neighbours*. London: Longmans, Green & Co., Ltd.

Moore, Harvey C., 1954, "Cumulation and Cultural Processes," *American Anthropologist*, n.s., 56:347–357.

Morgan, Lewis H., 1877, *Ancient Society*. New York: Henry Holt and Company, Inc.

Mulvaney, D. J., 1966, "The Prehistory of the Australian Aborigine," *Scientific American* 214:84–93.

Osgood, Cornelius, 1937, "The Ethnography of the Tanaina," *Yale University Publications in Anthropology*, no. 16.

————, 1940, "Ingalik Material Culture," *Yale University Publications in Anthropology*, no. 22.

Oswalt, Wendell H., 1955, "Prehistoric Sea Mammal Hunters at Kaflia, Alaska," *Anthropological Papers of the University of Alaska* 4:23–61.

————, 1967, *Alaskan Eskimos*. San Francisco: Chandler Publishing Company.

————, and VanStone, James W., 1967, "The Ethnoarcheology of Crow Village, Alaska," *Bureau of American Ethnology, Bulletin* 199.

Peckham, George W., and Peckham, Elizabeth G., 1898, "On the Instincts and Habits of the Solitary Wasps," *Wisconsin Geological and Natural History Survey*, Bulletin no. 2.

Pitt Rivers, Lane Fox, 1858, "On the Improvement of the Rifle as a Weapon for General Use," *Journal of the United Service Institution*, vol. 2, no. 8, 453–493.

Radcliffe-Brown, Alfred R., 1948, *Andaman Islanders* New York: The Free Press.

Robinson, George A., 1966, *Friendly Mission*, N. J. B. Plomley, ed. Kingsgrove, New South Wales: Tasmanian Historical Research Association.

Roth, Walter B., 1897, *Ethnological Studies among the North-West-Central Queensland Aborigines*. London: Queensland Agent-General's Office.

Rudenko, S. I., 1961, "The Ancient Culture of the Bering Sea and the Eskimo Problem," *Arctic Institute of North America, Anthropology of the North, Translations from Russian Sources* no. 1.

Sayce, R. U., 1965, *Primitive Arts and Crafts*. New York: Biblo and Tannen (originally published in 1933).

Schaller, George B., 1961, "The Orang-utan in Sarawak," *Zoologica* 46:73–82.

————, 1963, *Mountain Gorilla*. Chicago: University of Chicago Press.

————, and Lowther, Gordon R., 1969, "The Relevance of Carnivore Behavior to the Study of Early Hominids," *Southwestern Journal of Anthropology* 25:307–341.

Semenov, S. A., 1964, *Prehistoric Technology*. London: Cory, Adams & Mackay.

Service, Elman R., 1960, "Kinship Terminology and Evolution," *American Anthropologist*, n.s., 62:747–763.

————, 1962, *Primitive Social Organization*. New York: Random House, Inc.

————, 1968, "The Prime-mover of Cultural Evolution," *Southwestern Journal of Anthropology* 24:396–409.

Spencer, Walter B., 1914, *Native Tribes of the Northern Territory of Australia*. London: Macmillan & Co. Ltd.

————, and Gillen, Frank J., 1927, *Arunta*. 2 vols. London: Macmillian & Co., Ltd.

Steward, Julian H., 1933, "Ethnography of the Owens Valley Paiute," *University of California Publications in American Archaeology and Ethnology*, vol. 33, no. 3.

————, 1955, *Theory of Culture Change*. Urbana: University of Illinois Press.

Stirling, E. C., 1896, "Anthropology," *Report on the Work of the Horn Scientific Expedition to Central Australia*, pt. 4.

Thalbitzer, William, 1914, "The Ammassalik Eskimo," *Meddelelser om Gronland*, vol. 39.

Tindale, Norman B., 1925–1928, "Natives of Groote Eylandt and of the West Coast of the Gulf of Carpentaria," *Records of the South Australian Museum* 3:61–132.

Tobias, Phillip V., 1964, "Bushman Hunter-gatherers: A Study in Human Ecology," in *Ecological Studies in Southern Africa*, D. H. S. Davis, ed. Hague: W. Junk Publ., pp. 67–99.

Turnbull, Colin M., 1965, "The Mbuti Pygmies: An Ethnographic Survey," *Anthropological Papers of the American Museum of Natural History* 50: pt. 3.

van Riet Lowe, C., 1945, "The Evolution of the Levallois Technique in South Africa," *Man* 45:49–59.

van Rippen, Bene, 1918, "Notes on Some Bushmen Implements," *American Anthropological Association Memoir*, vol. 5, no. 3, 75–97.

Wagner, Philip L., 1960, *Human Use of the Earth*. New York: The Free Press.

Wallace, Anthony F. C., 1961, "On Being Just Complicated Enough," *Proceedings of the National Academy of Sciences* 47:458–464.

Webster's Third New International Dictionary, 1961, Philip B. Gove, ed. Springfield, Mass.: G. & C. Merriam Company.

White, Leslie A., 1949, *Science of Culture*. New York: Grove Press, Inc.

Williston, S. W., 1892, "Notes on the Habits of Ammophila," *Entomological News* 3:85–86.

Wolberg, Donald L., 1970, "The Hypothesized Osteodontokeratic Culture of the Australopithecinae: A Look at the Evidence and the Opinions," *Current Anthropology* 11:23–30.

Wolf, Eric R., 1964, "The Study of Evolution," in *Horizons of Anthropology*, Sol Tax, ed. Chicago: Aldine Publishing Co., pp. 108–119.

Znamierowska-Pruffer, Maria, 1966, *Thrusting Implements for Fishing in Poland and Neighboring Countries*. Warsaw: Scientific Publications Foreign Cooperation Center.